I0135442

ATROPOS PRESS
new york • dresden

General Editor:
Wolfgang Schirmacher

Editorial Board:
Giorgio Agamben
Pierre Alferi
Hubertus von Amelunxen
Alain Badiou
Judith Balso
Judith Butler
Diane Davis
Chris Fynsk
Martin Hielscher
Geert Lovink
Larry Rickels
Avital Ronell
Michael Schmidt
Fredrich Ulfers
Victor Vitanza
Siegfried Zielinski
Slavoj Žižek

© 2015 by Alain Badiou
Think Media EGS Series is supported by the European Graduate School

ATROPOS PRESS
New York • Dresden

151 First Avenue # 14, New York, N.Y. 10003

all rights reserved

978-1-940813-85-1

What is Philosophy?
A lecture by Alain Badiou
2010

Alain Badiou
Edited by Srdjan Cvjeticanin

How mad would he have to be to say, "He beheld
An order and thereafter he belonged
To it"? He beheld the order of the northern
sky.

But the beggar gazes on calamity
And thereafter he belongs to it, to bread
Hard found, and water tasting of misery.

For him cold's glacial beauty is his fate.
Without understanding, he belongs to it
And the night, and midnight, and after, where
it is.

What was he? What he has he has. But what?
It is not a question of captious repartee.
What has he that becomes his heart's strong
core?

He has his poverty and nothing more.
His poverty becomes his heart's strong core –
A forgetfulness of summer at the pole.

Sordid Melpomene, why strut bare boards,
Without scenery or lights, in the theatre's
bricks,
Dressed high in heliotrope's inconstant hue,

The muse of misery? Speak loftier lines.
Cry out, "I am the purple muse." Make sure
The audience beholds you, not your gown.

Wallace Stevens, *In a Bad Time*

Table of Contents

Editor's Note

The lecture transcribed below was given by Alain Badiou in the summer of 2010, over the course of six days, at the European Graduate School. The problem at stake was to think philosophy – its definition, its universal operation. This was not the first time Badiou addressed this question. Indeed, 'what is philosophy', had already been taken up in numerous written texts. For instance, in the Introduction to *Being and Event*, we find maybe the most condensed articulation: philosophy circulates between ontology, theories of the subject and its own history. There are also two short text included in *Conditions* and *Manifesto for Philosophy*, titled *Definition of Philosophy*, and *The (Re)turn of Philosophy Itself –* both of which must be read with the above definition. In addition to these explicit accounts there are numerous remarks throughout the edifice: in *Metapolitics* for instance, as well as in *Polemics*, *Ethics*, *Handbook of Inaesthetics*, and etc. Finally, following the thesis of Truth as the compossibility of truths and ontology, it must affirmed that the full definition of the Badiouian philosophy is found in *Being and Event*, from cover to cover – the other half of which is *Logics of Worlds*. Nonetheless, this lecture constitutes the longest explicit meditation on this reflexive question.

In fact, within this lecture we find a number of novel articulations of this deceptively difficult operation to define. For instance, Badiou here proposes that there are five conditions for the birth of philosophy, that philosophy has a very peculiar relation to time – including its own past – that it is oriented towards the future, and charged with aiding its production by way of a new collective desire, that it is structurally distinct from other forms of thought, such as nihilism and mysticism, and so on. That said, everything proposed in these lectures is nonetheless consistent with the doctrine introduced in *Being and Event*, and its supplements.

If I may, I would like to draw attention to a single proposition within these lectures: as one of the conditions of the birth of philosophy, Badiou – in apparent paradox – proposes the presence of the philosopher. The idea of the presence of a master as constitutive of the philosophical operation, in fact, returns a number of times throughout. For instance, the asymmetrical positions of the philosopher and student, the distinction of philosophy from other forms of thought, and, of course, it operates in style throughout. My reason for mentioning this is two-fold: it points at the apparently odd remark in *Being and Event* that a profound question of philosophy is the measure in which an event determines its fidelity, a curiosity found also in Badiou's remark that the trial of truth, and so, also Truth, cannot be endured without encountering the voice of a master, and second, the context of struggle within which Badiou proposes this idea. It could be added that from within the concept of truth, mastery at the beginning, no less than at the end, appears contradictory or even impossible. Certainly, with Badiou we do not stand in Kant or Lacan, but we do hear an echo of 'think and obey'. These Two, it must be wagered, do not stand to one another as two feet planted still, but as the walk of a march – which is also the walk of love.

This lecture was spoken in English, with only marginal notes. In view of these facts, I have here transcribed Badiou's lecture word for word, and assumed the liberty of editing his thought with the sole aim of trying to maintain the rhythm, the style, without overly compromising the exact sequence of words. I have made only minimal adjustments, and in all such cases any mistakes are mine.

March, 2015,
Srdjan Cvjetićanin

Ce texte provient de notes prises par des étudiants lors de mon séminaire de l'été 2010 à l'European Graduate School. C'est donc le reflet d'une exposition orale, souvent improvisée, et qui ne correspond à aucun texte écrit existant. Je n'ai pas relu ces notes, car j'aurais eu envie de tout réécrire, ce qui n'était pas dans l''esprit de cette tentative. Par conséquent, tout usage et toute citation de ce texte devra être accompagnée d'une indication précise de sa provenance, de façon à ce que personne ne puisse penser que je l'ai écrit ou revu.

This text is based on notes taken by students during the seminar I presented at the European Graduate School in the summer of 2010. It then reflects an oral contribution, with some degree of improvisation, and does not correspond to any written text. I did not re-read these notes as this would have lead me to a complete rewriting, which would not have been consistent with the initial spirit of this seminar. Consequently, any use or quotation of this text will have to be accompanied with a precise indication of its origin, so that nobody could think that I have either written or proof-read it.

A.B.

What is Philosophy?
A lecture by Alain Badiou
2010

Alain Badiou
Edited by Srdjan Cvjeticanin

1. Day One

1.1 Lecture I

Good morning to all of you!

I will begin with three very concrete problems. The first problem: why must we speak English? It is a real question, after all. It is the particularity of our world that everywhere we must speak English. It is an intellectual form of economic globalization, and also a philosophical form of economic globalization.

There is one world, *in some sense.* And, if really there is one world, then there is one language of this world. English is the language of our world, in some sense, but this is a problem too. It's a problem because philosophy is also the consideration of all difference, of the multiplicity of cultures and so on. Can we speak this one language – being inside globalization – and *accept the unity of this world,* which is the world today, but not necessarily a good world? After all, maybe its not a good world? Must philosophy be inside the world? It must, in some sense. It must because it is it's world, this world of today! It's a real problem.

We shall examine in detail this very interesting question. Not the general and objective question of globalization, as a characteristic of our world today, but the more specific question of the relationship between philosophy and this situation. The question 'why we must speak English' is only an aspect of this very massive problem of the relationship between the philosophical determination, which is also something like the subjective determination, and an objective situation, which, finally, is for us an obligation, the obligation to speak English, here, in Saas-fee. But if the European Graduate School was in Taiwan or Africa we would speak English too, and so it is not a question of this specific place, its a question of the world, of the totality.

It's also a paradoxical question – 'why we speak this language' – because it's not an historical result for philosophy itself. We can say something like this: philosophy has been written in three languages, principally Greek, French and German. Or, somewhat dogmatically, we can say: there is no philosophy which has been written in English. If we globalize the history of philosophy, from the beginning to today, we can say: the three major languages of philosophy have been Greek, French and German, certainly. And so, English is not a philosophical obligation, not at all. It would be, certainly, more interesting to speak Greek, for example, and it would be more difficult, for me as well – much more difficult than to speak English, and to speak English is very difficult for me, but to speak Greek is probably more difficult.

Finally, the result is here as a question: we must speak English, but why? Principally because we must *today* address philosophy to other people, to everybody, finally, and *today* everybody as such speaks English. In fact it's not true in everyday life, naturally – in everyday life we speak French and German, and, as you know, Chinese is certainly, in everyday life, more important than English. But, at the philosophical level, *today*, to address philosophy to other people we must speak English, we must be translated into English and so on. For example, when I speak to Chinese people we speak English.

So, we must. And so I want to say some words concerning my English. The American poet Wallace Stevens, says – somewhere – that French and English are in fact the same language. And it's true of the English of Wallace Stevens, and it's true of something French, it's a poetical characteristic of Stevens. For me, this was good news – French and English are the same language – but it was not my conviction. But, if a great poet says something like that, then maybe it's true. So my English is something like French dressed up as English, or French disguised into English. But the problem is that I cannot speak that sort of English, because it's French, in fact – in the sense of Wallace Stevens. So it's something like poetic English. But the problem is that very often it's very difficult for me to understand your English. Which is not, generally, French dressed up as English, but much more – it's difficult to say pure English – something much nearer to English, than mine. And, I can say, finally: your English is not enough French.

And so, as a consequence, I propose to you to give me, principally – not only, but principally – written questions. And so, finally, it's a concrete problem, in some sense. You will give me written questions, and I shall answer these questions and open a discussion concerning your questions during two lessons here: the second part of the afternoon tomorrow and the day after. You will write your name on the question. You have two complete lessons to discuss your questions. This would be the best possible organization of the collective discussion in a place where we have many people.

That is the first concrete problem. But it's not only a concrete problem it's also a very profound problem, which is the relationship *today* – *in this world* – between philosophy and universality. Is the universality of philosophy precisely its inscription, its presence, in the world as it is? Another possibility is that philosophy is universal precisely because it is not completely inside the world as it is, that philosophy is in a world, which, in some sense, does not exist. 'Does not exist' not because this world is a pure fiction, although that is a possibility

– many people, in fact, are saying that philosophy is useless or that it is nothing precisely because the world of philosophy does not exist. Can we not say the reverse: philosophy is useful because the world of philosophy is not exactly the world as it is, but something which is between the world as it is and the world as it must be. And, in fact, that this is how the world desires. So, the place of philosophy is between something realistic, the world as it is – and we must know the world as it is, we must understand the world as it is, we must propose something like a clear vision of the world as it is – and the point of view of something else, the point of view of the world not exactly as it is, from the position of what a sort of desire says concerning the world. This is the first question.

The second question – which is a consequence of the first – is: what exactly is the question of language in philosophy? Not only the abstract question of the structure of languages, the grammatical question, the logical question and so on, but the precise question of: in which language does philosophy exist? It's a very difficult question because there are today two possibilities. The first possibility is that today philosophy exists in the dominant language of globalization, that philosophy accepts being inside the world as it is, and so speaks the universal language of today, which is a sort of English in fact, not a pure English, but a sort of jargon. It's the first possibility, and there is something like an obligation to do something like that. I am a pure example: I speak to you in English. I am a proof of the necessity of that sort of inscription of philosophy in the world as it is. But I think that we cannot do only that, it's not a real creative possibility, after all. The creative possibility is to inscribe philosophy in the multiplicity of languages.

But what does it mean to say that philosophy is inside the difference of languages? It's not reducible to one language, because if philosophy is reducible to one language, and can be expressed only in this particular language, then it cannot be universal, certainly. There is this temptation. For example, Heidegger has explicitly said that German is today the real language of philosophy – after Greek, after Ancient Greek – and so that *being speaks German*. And, you know, this is in some sense a purely nationalist position, and now, finally, we can also say that it is something like a fascist position. I think that Heidegger is a great philosopher, but this position, this specific position concerning the language of philosophy, is absolutely against the universality of philosophy, against the recognition that something exists which is humanity as such, and not only humanity in the form of a specific language, a specific culture and so on. We'll return to this problem, which is not so simple.

Philosophy, in my sense – it's my condition – is not possible if we don't recognize that there exists something like humanity as such. Naturally, there are many cultures and differences and so on and so on, and humanity as such is a pure multiplicity in some sense, but this multiplicity is also something which must be recognized in its unity, in its fundamental unity. There is something like – to take a more technical word – a generic humanity: a humanity which is a humanity as such, and not reducible, not immediately reducible, to its immanent differences, or to any particularity.

If you say that philosophy speaks only one language, you can do that in two different meanings. The first meaning: we must speak English, not because being speaks English – poor being... – German, Ancient Greek and so on, not because of this technical reason, not because being speaks English, but because in the world as it is we must speak English. But *this is a necessity of today*, and not a metaphysical necessity – you understand that. Or, the other position – the position which is the position of Heidegger, but has also been the position of Leibniz, and so it's really something important in German history – is: we must speak English for ontological reasons, because there is something fundamental in the relationship between being as such and that language.

But these two possibilities are not good possibilities for philosophy. The first one, because there is something abstract in the fact of speaking English. I understand, of course, that it is a necessity to speak English in business, but the law of philosophy cannot be exactly the law of business, after all – philosophy is not a business. This is a question for philosophy today, *because today everything is business.* And so the question is: is philosophy today able to be an exception? And this is a great question in philosophy, this question of: does there exist something like a philosophical exception? We cannot be reduced to the laws of business, we cannot be reduced to the idea of being speaking one language and not the others. Sometimes, however, this idea that we must speak *only* our specific language is what is opposed to the abstract idea of everyone having to speak English. This, in fact, is a form of the main contradiction of today: the contradiction of nationalist reaction against globalization…. *It's a possibility*, and it is also, *in some sense*, a philosophical possibility. It would not exactly be a properly philosophical position, but we could affirm that because we cannot accept to speak the common business language, which is English, we must speak only our proper language, our language of ordinary life and so on.

Sometimes I think that the major risk concerning philosophy is to be structured by this sort of contradiction: on one side abstract universality, in the form of globalization and business, and on the other side a sort of nationalistic reaction, which assumes that we must be absolutely closed in our particularity. This is something which concerns the contemporary world. Naturally, my conviction is that we must go beyond this opposition, we must say that there is something like universality, that there is something like the unity of the world, the unity of humanity as such, and, on the other side, we must recognize, completely, the differences, including the differences of languages. But to go beyond the contradiction is a dialectical problem.

How is it possible to resolve that sort of contradiction? It is, I think, the most important contradiction of the world today: the contradiction of abstract universality, which is, finally, the universality of imperialism, the universality of business, capitalism and so on, and the formal language of this process is English, and, on the other side, the reaction of different cultures against this abstract universality, but in the form of the pure affirmation of their particularity. It's a great difficulty for philosophy today, because the fidelity to the history of philosophy as such is always to propose to move beyond that sort of closure, the closure between abstract universality, purely abstract universality, which is an oppressive universality, a universality against the life of different people and so on, and a purely reactive particularity, which affirms the particularity as such, in a fight against abstract universality. We can understand that sort of fight, but there is no possibility for philosophy to be inscribed purely in that sort of opposition. And so, philosophy can affirm neither the abstract vision of the world of globalization – our peaceful world of business – nor the obscure position of Heidegger – "being speaks German". If you want: neither 'business speaks English, so we must speak English', nor 'I am a German and so I must speak German and nothing else'.

This is, also – I think – a political contradiction, naturally, and not only a philosophical one or a cultural one. It's a political opposition between something like the political position on the side of globalization, which assumes, which affirms, that globalization, business, English and so on, are the destiny of humanity, *the only possibility of humanity*, and the absolute affirmation of particularity. The philosophical name of the first of these political positions is abstract universality. Abstract universality is the political position that the Western World is the paradigm for the history of all humanity, that we have today a single possibility, a single political possibility, which is, finally, the expansion, the universal expansion, of the world as it is – it is, simply put, the affirmation that the world as it is is the only possibility of the world as it is. It is a political position to say something like that. To say 'we are inside a world of which the only possibility is the continuation of this world as it is,' naturally with something a little better, something a little more green, and so on, is a political position which, at the global level, affirms that the future of the world as it is is, in some sense, the world as it is, and not something else – 'something else' in a radical sense.

This political position is the real conservative one today. The true enemy today – I speak in the vocabulary of war – the true enemy is absolutely not the obscure position, because it's not the dominant position. The obscure position exists, and it is an enemy too, but the true enemy is much more the position that we must continue purely and simply, that we must continue, that there is no possibility for the world other than to continue the world as it is, that we have nothing to do other than continue the world as it is. *This* position is also the position that the worlds as it is is the peace of business... the peace of business, which is, as you know, imposed in some parts of the world by war... the war to impose on everybody the peace of business.

I insist on the point that *this* position is the true conservative one today: generally we name the 'conservative position' what is, in fact, the obscure position. A position which affirms that we must return to the old world, to 'family', to old laws – for instance concerning freedom of sexuality, and so on – that we must return under the law of God and to the old world with its rites and so on and so on. Naturally, this obscure position is something dangerous and something horrible, and we must act against all that, but it's not the true fundamental enemy at the end. It is something like a reaction against the true conservative position, which is, the reactive position, and which claims that we must continue the process of the world as it is and that we have no other possibility. *This* is the position of practically all governments of the great countries today – the great countries of Europe, the United States, China and so on. They have contradictions, differences between them, as always, but they have something in common, which is fundamental: they all affirm that we have finished with proposing completely new visions of this world *as possibilities of this world,* not as fictions, not as utopias, but as possibilities which are *real possibilities of the world as it is. That... that is the first tendency, the dominant tendency, of today*: the affirmation that the world as it is has no true possibility inside itself other than to continue the world as it is. And that is, in fact, the definition – the philosophical definition – of the conservative position, which I have named the reactive position.

On the other side of the contradiction, we have today, probably, only the obscure position, and *this* – that these are the only two possibilities – *this* is the danger of our situation. The obscure position is not 'the continuation of the world as it is, the continuation of the good world', but the position that we must return to something which is in the form of the old world, which is, as we know, a religious reaction, some form of radical Islam, and so on, but also Bush, and by some respects, my dear Sarkozy, and, in Italy, Berlusconi, and so on. Finally, the obscure position is – in my vision of the political world – only something like the reverse of the reactive one, but which is inside the conservative one.

The dominant conservative position affirms the necessity to continue the world as it is, and the obscure one says that we must desire the world of the past, the same world, but of the past. And so, I think the dominant idea today on one side and on the other side, of both the conservative position and the obscure position is: no real future, no real future.

If the only possibility of the world is to continue the world as it is, then there is no real future, no real future. What is a real future? A real future is something different. If we do not have the possibility of something different, then we do not have a real future, we have, rather, a continuation of the present, a sort of enormous present. And this is the time of today: the time of today is to reduce time to the pure present, to the continuation, to the transformation, the immanent transformation of the present as such. *This* is why we have the philosophical affirmation of 'the end of history', the classical idea, which is, in some sense, a Hegelian idea: we are at the end, the world as it is is the world. And, if the world as it is must continue the world as it is, its, in fact, the end of history, it's the abolition of the future.

To finish with this first concrete problem – 'why we must speak English' – I can say: if philosophy is really useful today, it is because philosophy must be on the side of the attempt to escape that sort of false contradiction – the contradiction between the conservative position and the reactive position. This is our contradiction, which is the dominant contradiction, but, finally, it is also a false contradiction, because there is something in common in that contradiction, which is, no future. No future because *if the world has no other possibility than itself, then there is no future.* And, *if the world has no desire other than a return to the past, then there is no future.* So we can define one goal of philosophy – if philosophy is something useful, if it is something else than an academic exercise, if philosophy is really something useful to our life: philosophy must propose the possibility of a real future, or to examine the conditions for the existence of a real future. This is the first concrete problem.

The second concrete problem is: what is our duty, our duty *here, in this room*? What are the duties of a professor and students? My duty, my duty as a professor, is to be with you for three hours a day during six days, six successive days. And we can say that, after all, it's a professional duty – my duty as professor is to be with you. What is your duty as students? It is also the duty to be with me, for three hours a day, for six days. But what sort of duty is that, finally? What sort of duty? It's not completely clear, and it's particularly not completely clear concerning this sort of university, because you are not exactly young students coming, finally, to become something in business, or in the world as it is – it's not exactly the situation here. You know that. So, your duty is not exactly a professional duty. It's a difference between you and me. It is possible for me to understand my duty in a purely professional manner but that's not exactly your case. There is something like a freedom of choice to be here.

My idea is that we can speak, *that we must speak*, of something like a philosophical duty, a duty not reducible to the interests of the human animal – to be in a business, to have money, to buy something, some products, to have a good life and so on and so on. A philosophical duty cannot be something like that.... And the point is that if your duty is of philosophical nature, if it is of philosophical nature, then it is, in some sense, a disinterested duty, it is a duty not reducible to your individual interests and nothing else. If this is the case – if there is this disinterestedness to you duty – then it is of philosophical nature, and not purely professional. And so, we have here again a dialectical situation.

This is the real situation of a class of philosophy, a real class of philosophy: there is a common duty that is of philosophical nature by itself, because it is not reducible to something else. And I must transform my duty into a philosophical one, and your duty as students is transformed into a philosophical duty too, in

some sense. And so, we constitute a philosophical community –
it is our ideal, maybe it's not exactly true, or always true, but it is
our ideal. And this constitution of a philosophical community is
a philosophical question. It's not the same as if you are here to
learn mathematics, for example. It's not identical. I know this
because I love mathematics and sometimes I transform myself
into a professor of mathematics, and immediately I can
understand that the community is not the same: it is not the same
because the dissymmetry in knowledge is not the same. We must
explain this – and it is our second concrete question: why is a
class of philosophy not the same thing as a class of geography,
of mathematics, and so on? It is, I think, because of the
dialectical nature of philosophy, form Plato to today.

The dialectical nature of philosophy produces a new form of the
relationship between the professor and the students. Why?
Because we must create, we must attempt to create – it can be a
failure, naturally – we must create something like a new
common desire. The question of philosophy is the question of
creating a new desire – it's not just to give answers to some
problems. Naturally we propose some answers to some
problems, but that is not the goal of philosophy. The goal of
philosophy is not like the goal in mathematics – to explain a
problem and a solution of the problem. The goal is not as it is in
empirical questions either – to learn something new, concerning
the geography of some country, or history and so on. It's not to
know the laws of the world, like in economy, for instance, and
so on. It is really to create *in everybody* a new desire. *And if we
create a new community, it is because there is something in
common* – and not only between the professor and students –
which is precisely the possibility of that sort of new desire. The
creation of that sort of new desire is of dialectical nature because
we are not – you and me – in the same position at the beginning,
we are different: I speak and you learn, you write and I speak,
and so on. It is not the same position, not at all. *But the goal is*

not to continue indefinitely that difference, in fact it is *to not continue that difference indefinitely*, the goal is to produce something common, which is precisely a new desire. And it is to produce this *as a result of this difference of position*!

As you immediately understand a new common desire is not exactly the same desire – there is something individual in a new desire. Everybody understands the situation in a different manner and so on. But what is in common is the problem of a new desire, *as the result of a philosophical process*. This is the case not only in a class, but also when you read the book of philosophy. If you *really* read a book of philosophy, that is, if your reading is of a philosophical nature, it's not to learn what there is in the book – naturally, very often its the case, because you have exams and so on, and you must learn something, and you read the book, and 'oh yeah, its a horrible book, its very difficult, and abstract, and so on' but all that is not of a philosophical nature, it is of an academic nature. What is of a philosophical nature when you read the book is *also* to open a new desire. And so, it is also something like a subjective transformation. This is the point. The question of philosophy is not a new knowledge, but a new desire. It's true from Plato to today – it is not a new idea.

And so the dialectical nature – we return to this point – of philosophy is that the goal of philosophy is not the production of knowledge and the accumulation of knowledge, but a qualitative subjective transformation, by way of the creation of a new common desire. The very nature of philosophy is here... the very nature of philosophy is here. Philosophy is not a knowledge, it is not an academic field, it is not books, and so on. Naturally, it is all that, but all that are means... they are just means, it is not the thing itself. Philosophy itself... philosophy itself is the process of subjective transformation. And if we must be together – you and me – during some hours and days, we can, naturally, say that it is because it is the program of the European Graduate School, for me and for you, finally – its true, its exact. But what is the norm of success, the norm of a victory, if you want, concerning this sort of situation? What is a victory here? The victory is not to come to know something that you did not know before – maybe there is something like that, but it's not the philosophical victory of the class. The collective victory of the class – which always includes you and me – is the emergence of something like a new desire, or a new possibility in thinking, a new vision. And this is a small part, a small part, but a part of the first question – the creation of a new collective future, the creation of a new possibility. But a new possibility begins by a new subjective position, because if we are subjectively reduced to the world as it is, then, naturally, we cannot support any new possibilities. This is why a class of philosophy, but also the reading by one person of a book of philosophy, has as a norm of success – of philosophical success – something like a small subjective transformation, which is a small part of the opening of new possibilities of the world itself.

This is a philosophical question because we must be conscious that when we have a new possibility, a new real possibility, *this is a part of the general problem of a new possibility*. And this is why philosophy is simultaneously purely individual and completely universal. It's purely individual because it's not politics – we don't create a philosophical organization, a philosophical party, that is a question of politics, properly. Everybody knows that the goal of philosophy is not to create a new political organization, a new revolutionary party, or something like that. Philosophy at its proper level is an individual question, it is really an individual question. It is, after all, the possibility of a new desire of somebody, and not of humanity as such. Humanity as such, in some sense, exists and does not exist. I cannot speak to humanity as such, but I can speak to you. And, certainly, you are a collection of individuals, but you are not a party or an organization – yes you are at European Graduate School, but European Graduate School is not a political party.

So I speak to you, that is, I speak to everybody in the class. Philosophy is purely individual, in some sense, and at this level there are differences, dissymmetries, and so on – my position, for example, is not the position of everyone in the class and so on. But if the goal of philosophy is a new desire concerning the world, if it is a new individual desire but a new desire concerning the world as it is, concerning a new possibility of life, a new possibility for existence, and not only a new knowledge of what is, then that sort of desire is also a part of a collective transformation. And we must understand, finally, that what is at question here is not the creation of a new future *but the creation of the possibility of a new future* – there is a difference, there is a difference between the two.

The dialectical nature of philosophy is that philosophy is the relationship between the individual and the world, in fact, it is the transformation of the relationship between the individual and the world, by the means of thinking, by means of a new desire in thinking, because thinking is also a question of desire, naturally.

At the beginning we have a big difference between the philosopher – or the book – and the individual, but the result – the goal – is the emergence of a new common desire concerning the relationships between individuals and the world. After that maybe there are some actions, some engagements and so on. But philosophy itself is the creation *of the possibility* of all that. And this possibility is made possible by way of a new subjective position of individuals.

Philosophy is one-by-one, and not a collective address, which is why a class is not a political meeting or something like that, but a class, a collection of individuals. Philosophy is one-by-one, really, but this one-by-one is not the closure of the one on itself, it is not the closure of the individual within himself or herself. On the contrary, it is the opening of the individual to something like a new possibility, which can be, and generally is, also a collective possibility, but a collectively possibility seen from the point of view of the individual.

Our first question concerns the dialectical nature of philosophy, the question is: what is philosophy? And this is, in fact, the old question of philosophy – 'what is philosophy'. And, in fact, this question – and that it is a philosophical question, that it is a question within philosophy itself – is a part of the dialectical nature of philosophy. As you know, the question 'what is mathematics?' is not a mathematical question. There is no theorem, no definition or proposition concerning the question 'what is mathematics' in mathematics. And the question 'what is painting?' is not a question in painting, and so on. But 'what is philosophy' *is a question of philosophy.* Philosophy is necessarily dialectal because the question of its proper nature is precisely one of its questions. There is something reflexive in philosophy, and it is always reflexive, and this reflexivity is not only the sense of psychological reflection and so on. No. There is something *objectively reflexive,* because the question of philosophy is a philosophical question. And this point is also connected to my affirmation that the goal of philosophy is to create a new desire. The two cannot be separate because if philosophy did not include the question of philosophy, then philosophy would be a knowledge, it would be a knowledge of something. And so my duty would be to transmit to you this sort of knowledge, like in mathematics or history and so on. If philosophy is something the goal of which is to create a new individual desire concerning the possibilities of the world, then, by necessity, philosophy is also the question of philosophy itself, and not a closed body of knowledge.

For philosophy to be the opening of the individual to a new desire we must have an opening of philosophy itself – if philosophy is closed it creates something closed, naturally. To create something open, philosophy must be open too, and the opening of philosophy is precisely that in philosophy we have the question of philosophy. Philosophy does not begin by 'I know what is philosophy, and, okay, I go'. No. Philosophy always begins by a question, it begins by the question 'what is philosophy'. This is why the question of Socrates is 'what is philosophy', explicitly. And my dear friend Deleuze, with Guattari, also wrote a book *What is Philosophy?* And so, at the very beginning and at the end we have 'what is philosophy'. And we know that the answer to this question is an answer which is itself open, and it must be open because the answer to the question is always the point of departure of another manner of forming the question. And so we have the repetition of this question across the history of philosophy, we have it across the entire history up until now. If you read Deleuze – the magnificent book, *What is Philosophy?* – you will see that it is just another possibility, another manner of putting the question 'what is philosophy'. And so the history of philosophy is also the history of the question concerning philosophy, absolutely. There is no ahistorical determination, no final determination, of the answer to 'what is philosophy', and then, after that, philosophy. No. There is a constant repetition of the question 'what is philosophy', and, naturally, there is something like a sequence of different answers to this question. And so, there is something absolutely open in philosophy. And it's a necessity because all forms of the closure of philosophy are also the death of philosophy, because the life of philosophy is the possibility of opening the thinking of individuals to new possibilities.

If philosophy must be something like that, then it is, in some sense, opposed to the world. It is opposed to the world because the dominant position in the world today is the conservative one, which is the affirmation that the only possibility of the world is to continue what it is. If philosophy is as we have proposed, then philosophy cannot be in accord with the world. And the opening of philosophy is not in accord with the conservative position, because philosophy itself is always saying that philosophy must be something else. And it is the fact of this question that explains why there exist philosophers, different philosophers. Why? Because there is a constant transformation not only of philosophy, but of the question 'what is philosophy', and the two, naturally, are not separate. And so philosophy *by itself* is already the affirmation of the possibility of something else. The continuation of philosophy, therefore, is not conservative, it cannot be conservative, the history of philosophy cannot be of the form of the continuation of a philosophy. Maybe we could even say that what continues is the question... the problem of philosophy.

And as you know every philosopher begins by saying 'I am writing something completely new'. Certainly it's not completely true, but we *cannot begin in any other manner*, we must begin all the works of philosophy by saying 'I propose something absolutely new'. The history of philosophy is not a history of continuity but a history of ruptures, the history of philosophy is a succession of ruptures. And the beginning itself is never the same – the beginning of Aristotle is not the beginning of Plato, and so on.

We must be clear on this point: if philosophy is something like that – a succession of ruptures – then there is, in fact, something revolutionary in philosophy itself. There is something revolutionary in philosophy itself because at the conceptual level it is the idea of a rupture in thinking, it is the idea of a new way. If there is always something like that in philosophy, then – and I return to this point – philosophy today is not in accord with the world because the *dominant vision of the world today is the conservative one*, which supposes that there is no other possibility than the development of the world as it is, that the final success of humanity is the democratic and capitalistic world. But philosophy is *not* compatible with the idea of a final success. There is no final success possible in philosophy, because philosophy cannot give a definite answer to 'what is philosophy'. Philosophy cannot give a definite answer to anything. Even concerning itself, philosophy cannot give a final answer, it cannot say what is philosophy and have it be the final success of that question.

But, *in some sense,* the conservative position exists in philosophy, and it consists in saying that philosophy is exactly like other knowledges – a succession of good problems and good answers. The name of this position, as you all know, is analytic philosophy. Analytic philosophy assumes the fact that philosophy must be rational – in a completely rigid sense of rational – and that philosophy must be a succession of problems collectively assumed, with good answers and bad answers, and so on. The result is, finally, that – in this sense of philosophy – you could have a professor of philosophy who says that all that is really important are the papers of the last ten years of philosophy. And in this sense it would be exactly like science, because in science what is important for the creative scientist are the papers of the last ten years, naturally. And so, we have today a conservative position in philosophy, which is the reduction of philosophy to collection of good problems, and a collection of good solutions. And so philosophy would not at all be a question of creating a new desire, a new future, or a new possibility.

Rather, philosophy would be something that is only concerned with being precise, with being in a field of knowledge – logical, grammatical, linguistic, and so on – with being a conceptual knowledge, with very clear rules, with very determined rules, with very clear positions, and a very clear and determined horizon. And this is a very strong position today, because it's position which is really inside the world as it is, it's a position which is in conformity with the world, a position which is not a succession of ruptures, but a collective and rational continuation of the same thing, of the same discipline. And so philosophy, in this case, would be completely reduced to an academic exercise. In which case it would be something that exists only and fully in universities, and something that is not addressed to humanity as such any more than geography, chemistry, or something like that. But we can see that that sort of position suppresses, that it abolishes, the dialectical nature of philosophy. And, finally, we can see that the name analytic philosophy is appropriate to this position, we can see that it is a good name, because in the tradition of philosophy there is precisely the opposition between dialectic and analytic.

Conceptually analytical is the contrary of dialectical. And so, the analytical position in philosophy is the abolition of the dialectical nature of philosophy, precisely by the affirmation that we know what is philosophy because we can define the rules and objectives of philosophy, and the proposition that all we can do and all the we must do is continue all of that. And this position is, consequently, also the suppression of the creative position of philosophy – in the sense of the existence of philosophers. Naturally, if you have good rules, good problems, good answers, you can work collectively, no problem – exactly like a laboratory of scientists.

There is a link, a relationship, between the question of 'what is philosophy', the dialectical nature of philosophy, the creation of new possibilities, the question of a new desire, and so on. But this knot is not the dominant position today, the dominant position is analytic philosophy, because it is in accord with the world, because it is inscribed in the world as it is. But we must also understand that this dominant position is also the closure of philosophy, the end of philosophy. This is the best definition of this position: to the question of philosophy we have an answer, a definite answer, exactly as we have a definite answer to what is the good world – the good world is the world as it is, with imperfections and defects, but the history will be a good one. And, finally, we must understand that these two answers are not separate... they are not separate... not at all.

And so, there is a fight, a real fight here – it is not a peaceful situation. We have a fight between these two positions, between the two possible general orientations of philosophy. There is, first, the dialectical position, which is the idea of philosophy as an open question, as a creation of a new desire, as something like the production of the idea of a future – it's not the creation of the future, the creation of the future is a political question, an artistic question, a question of action, of creation, and so on, but the creation of the idea of a future, of the possibility of a future. The conservative position, on the other hand, is the attempt of a closure of philosophy, exactly like the attempt of the closure of the world. In this vision we have the impossibility of a true rupture with this vision. Maybe, at the very abstract level, the question of today is the contradiction between the analytic vision and the dialectical vision. It's certainly the contradiction in philosophy.

We can probably generalize this vision. In philosophy it is clear, it is absolutely clear. Sometimes this contradiction has been called the contradiction between continental philosophy and analytic philosophy, but it is more complex than that. We can generalize because philosophy is – and this is another possible definition of philosophy – a symptom, a symptom of the world, because the divisions in philosophy are always also divisions in the world itself. And today – probably – in all fields of creation the fight is between opening and closure, between the dialectical vision and the analytical vision. Certainly this is the stake in philosophy, *but philosophy is a symptom of something much more important.* And in politics it is clear as well: reactive politics and obscure politics are both different forms of closure, and the question is whether there is another possibility, a third possibility. The war today between the Western World and 'terrorism' is, in fact, a war between two forms of closure. We must see this! We must see that they are both forms of closure. Ultimately, this war is a war between closure by the continuity of the present and closure by a return to the past. But a closure by a return to the past and a closure by a continuity of the present have something in common, something very important, which is that there is no future, no true future, that there is no other possibility. The true contradiction, however, is that the formal contradiction is based on an excluded third possibility. And so what we have today is a conservative war, in some sense. And what is horrible is not only that it's a war, but that it's a war between two false visions.

In philosophical terms we can say that in this war both positions are analytical, and not dialectical: it is a war between two analytical positions, between two positions which are both closed, between two positions neither of which is an opening to the future. And both are, finally, of a defensive nature: it is not the creation of something new, but of a choice between a return and a continuation. To this position we can oppose the dialectical nature of philosophy, and its affirmation of the necessity of a new future, its affirmation of the possibility of a new possibility, its affirmation that in the world as it is we must open the possibility of another world, and that this possibility cannot be just a fiction but a real possibility – I insist on this point. And we must absolutely resist the common affirmation that philosophy, radical political visions, and so on are pure fictions, fantasies, or senseless propositions. Such affirmations are a part of the war, they are a part of the ideological war, they are instruments against the idea of the possibility of a new possibility. And they are false, they are not true, finally, they are not true because the possibility of a new possibility is a not just a possibility.

Our philosophical problem is not to propose a sort of closed fiction, a pure utopia. A utopia is a closed fiction, after all: it is another sort of closure, because if you say that the world as it is is not good and you propose a pure fiction of another world which does not exist, and which is not a possibility of our future, then you are also in a closure, a negative closure but a closure.

With such a proposal we would not be in the conservative position – the only possibility of the world is the world as it is – nor in the obscure position – the world is not good, and we must return to an old world – but we would be proposing a pure phantasmagoria, a pure fiction, a pure phantasm of the world. The question is of the possibility *inside the world* of something that is really different – *that is our problem*. If something like *that* does not exist, then the dialectical position of philosophy would be void, it is true. And so, the analytical camp would be victorious, and it would be the end of history. And, finally, it is my position that this would be the end of everything which is of interest, because it would be the end of the idea of creation... the end of the idea of creation... it would be the end of artistic creation, the end of scientific creation – because science becomes the slave of technology and business – it would be the end of love as a creative position of existence as such, it would be the end of all that is rupture, of all that is creative, of all that is true in human existence. It is a position, a horrible position.

In some sense the only norm of the conservative vision is security. The dialectical position, on the other hand, involves the acceptance of some risk – certainly you cannot have the dialectical position and pure security, it's impossible, you must accept some risk. We perfectly know that we cannot have perfect security with love, for example – I take this example because its the most common. When we are engaged in true love we cannot expect pure security, it's absolutely impossible. And it's the same thing when you are in artistic experimentation: when you want to create something new, a new critique of some forms, and so on, you cannot say 'ah, yes, but I desire absolute security, no failure, only success!', that would be absurd, naturally. But *that is* the reactive vision. The most important name in the conservative vision is security. In politics this is clear, but the other fields too are under the law of security. And the analytic position is philosophy with security. That is another possible definition: analytic philosophy is philosophy with complete security, complete predictabilty, a philosophy of only good problems and good answers.

This is the great fight of the contemporary world: analytical vision and dialectical vision, security or creativity. The problem is that the position of the analytic vision – security, continuation of the world as it is – is a very strong position, it is a very strong position because humanity as such is divided, humanity as such loves security, it demands security. This fight is a fight inside subjectivity itself.

As you all know, Socrates was condemned to death because philosophy is the corruption of young people. But what is 'corruption of young people'? It is precisely to teach them that security is not the true desire of humanity, and it is to propose to them a dialectical vision, a vision where we assume some part of risk, some part of chance, some part of uncertainty, and also the desire of difference and not the very powerful demand of sameness. And it is clear, it is absolutely clear that the fundamental demand of the contemporary world is for sameness, for the identical, for continuation, for the continuation of itself. Philosophical corruption showed that philosophy is something completely different from all of that, and that philosophy has a desire that is different from that of the contemporary world.

This is our second problem, and so, naturally, we have two possibilities concerning our class. I have an idea, a goal for this class, a goal for what I am doing here, but it is only one possibility, it is only one possibility out of two. There is, first, the analytic possibility – I can give you some new knowledge, I can show you some good problems and good answers – and there is the dialectical possibility. But this possibility involves some risk – not the risk of death, and maybe not the risk of love – it involves the risk of a modification, the risk of a transformation, maybe a small transformation, a very small transformation, but a rupture, a small rupture in the subjective position of our community.

We stop, finally.

We have examined the first two concrete problems. The first was to decide why we must speak English. As we saw, the true meaning of this small question is the anthropological situation of philosophy, which is philosophy's relationship to the world, to the concrete world, to the questions of culture, globalization, languages and so on. Abstractly, the question is: how is it that philosophy is not reducible to anthropological determination? The key of the problem is the notion of possibility. You understand why? Possibility is something which is inside and outside: it is inside because the possibility must exist *in the world*, but it is also outside because if something is possible and not realized its not exactly in the world. The first question, therefore, is the relationship between philosophy and possibility.

The second concrete question was the problem of our role here, of our duty, of what we must do in the concrete situation of this room. The general problem of this question is the dialectical nature of philosophy, and the proposition between this dialectical nature of philosophy and the conservative vision of analytical philosophy. We have seen – without detail – that this contradiction is a symptom, a philosophical symptom, of what is probably the most important contradiction of the contemporary world, the contradiction between the analytic and the dialectic vision.

We have seen that all of that is a part of the question 'what is philosophy'. I will give you three possible short references for reading concerning this question, and the repetition, the very strange repetition of this question from the beginning of philosophy to today: I think its possible to read - its just a suggestion, not an obligation – *What is Metaphysics?*, of Heidegger, *What is Philosophy?*, of Deleuze and Guattari, and my *Manifesto for Philosophy* – if you accept a narcissistic indication.

We can now, finally, name our third concrete problem, which is very, very concrete: why is there this sort of situation where an old man speaks to much younger people? As you know the philosophical form transforms everything into a question! But we must understand in what sense it is a question.

Probably you know that I am seventy-three years old, and so my historical existence includes the Second World War, the Chinese Revolution, the imperialist wars in Algiers, Vietnam, and so on, May '68 in France, Roosevelt, Churchill, de Gaulle, Stalin, but also Kennedy, Castro, Che Guevara and so on. And my historical existence is an important part of.... Certainly, we can say that my historical world, the concrete becoming of this world – the different events, the ruptures, the continuities and so on – is not same as yours. And my philosophical framework is specific, naturally. For example, it implies Sartre, Heidegger, and also – directly, not as something finished, but as something in becoming – Derrida, Foucault, Lacan, Deleuze and so on. I can say, if you want, that my life goes across practically four sequences concerning philosophy.

I can give you a sort of approximate knowledge of this history. During the '50's, of the last century, the dominant position in Europe was phenomenology – Husserl, Heidegger, Sartre, Merleau-Ponty, and so on – and the most important concept was the question of consciousness, or subjectivity. And, maybe, the most important question was 'what exactly is freedom'. And in that sort of context the discussion was between phenomenology, on one side, and on the other side – as the conservative position, if you want – was positivism, philosophy of sciences and so on. It was in this contradiction that, as a young man, I was in my first contact with philosophy.

Immediately after that we have something very different the name of which in France was structuralism – the English name was French Theory. In the '60's and part of the '70's the dominant position was structuralism, that is, a philosophy of structure, a philosophy of objective structures and also philosophy of language. Naturally, this moment was a critique of the previous moment of philosophy, and so it was a critique of the concept of subject and a critique of consciousness as the most important concepts in philosophy. We find something like this, for example, in the critique of the concept of humanity by Foucault, or in the critique of the concept of subjectivity by Althusser, and so on. Certainly structuralism was largely a critique of phenomenology – in fact, it is often the case that what succeeds is a critique of what is succeeded. And for me, naturally, this passage was a difficulty because I was really Sartrean – I was on the side of consciousness – and so it was very difficult for me to go across a radical critique of consciousness, and to accept the apology of structure and the determination of the subject by language and so on.

After that we have something like a third sequence – purely in philosophy, the political sequences are different – during the '80's and '90's, which is the sequence of deconstruction and post-modernity. It was the idea of something like the end of philosophy, not in the analytic sense of closure, but in the sense that philosophy itself is too closed. It was the idea that the opening of classical philosophy was a form of closure, and that the name of this closure was metaphysics, naturally.

There was something Heideggerian in this sequence, because it was the sequence of the end of philosophy as the end of metaphysics. But – as Derrida also learned – to say 'the end' is too much, because 'the end' itself is a closure! And so it is the end of the end! It was the continuation of the end, it was the end without end, the end which does not end. This is why deconstruction is infinite. Deconstruction is infinite because the end of metaphysics must also be the deconstruction of deconstruction. It was, certainly, the idea of a radical opening, of an absolute opening. Not absolute as the end of thinking, as the goal of thinking, but the absolute as the realization of the end, a realization itself infinite. Deconstruction, then, was a radical critique of some aspects of the sequence before, because the sequence before was *constructivist* – structuralism is constructivism, and it was the idea that you could understand the thing itself by its structure. The sequence of post-modernity and deconstruction is the sequence of the critique of that sort of constructivism, because it proposed that the idea of construction is a closure. But it also proposed the same for deconstruction, and so it was necessary to deconstruct not only the construction, but also the deconstruction of the deconstruction, and so on. It was the idea of an infinite task, an infinite obligation, of something without immanent end – in fact, it was the first appearance of this idea in the history of philosophy. Another aspect of this sequence was to assume all of the past. In the field of art this assumption is very clear, it is very clear because in art today we have a sort of game with all forms, all historical forms, precisely because we are not obliged to the new form and only the new form.

During this sequence there is also a powerful academic reaction. Maybe it is not true for the whole of the Anglo-Saxon world, but at least in the United States and England the contradiction during this sequence was a contradiction between deconstruction and analytic philosophy, strictly speaking. But philosophers like Deleuze and I were outside of this contradiction, we were outside because our positions were neither that of post-modernity – like the position of Lyotard for example, but also many others – nor that of analytic philosophy. We were not on the side of Derrida, but we were not on the side of the enemies of Derrida either, and so we were in some sense outside the contradiction, outside the violent contradiction of this sequence.

After that – after the contradiction between deconstruction and post-modernity and the academic reaction – we have something like a new sequence which is probably still obscure and not yet completely clear. The English word for this sequence is post-post-modernity... post-post-modernity. Is it possible that the sequence after this is post-post-post-modernity? I can understand what is post-post-modernity in the sense that we return to some concepts of classical philosophy without being an academic reaction. That is my definition of something like that. We are not in deconstruction and post-modernity, because we can assume that some metaphysical concepts like being, subject, truth and so on, are valid. And so, naturally, it appears as if we have returned to classical metaphysics, but it is not the case, it is not exactly the case for Deleuze or for me. But there is no problem in assuming that our position is a metaphysical one, because, precisely, we are not in the field of the deconstruction of metaphysical concepts. The idea is precisely to assume some classical concepts of metaphysics but without being a return to the metaphysical sequence of the history of philosophy. And so, naturally, we must give new meanings to all classical concepts – I will return to this problem later. This is why I understand post-post-modernity in this sense: it is not post-modernity, it is not deconstruction, or freedom in the game of forms and so on, it is not an absolute negation of metaphysics, of all the concepts of classical metaphysics, such as subject, truth, etc., but it is not a return to classical metaphysics either. Equally, post-post-modernity is not in the analytic and academic reaction to all of that either. We are beyond that contradiction, and to be beyond that contradiction means that we are in a new sequence. Maybe its the sequence of post-post-modernity, I can accept the name.

So, we can say that all that constitutes four sequences in the fifty, sixty years of my life.

I can add something else: during practically the entirety of the first two sequences we have two fundamental references, Marxism and psychoanalysis, Marx and Freud, if you want. Everybody who was in the phenomenological framework – in the sense of Sartre or Merleau-Ponty – and also everybody who was in the field of structuralism, has these two major references. There is something in Marxism and psychoanalysis that is *not reducible* to the succession of sequences, and which cuts across all of them. In fact, even in the third sequence somebody like Derrida is in constant discussion with Freud and Marx – Derrida wrote about Marx directly, a book, an entire book. It is very important to see that in European philosophy, in continental philosophy, Marxism and psychoanalysis go cross the three first sequences. which are, on other points, very different, very exclusive.

At the end of these three sequences there was a very strong reaction against these two references. In France, this reaction took the form of the New Philosophers. Today, in fact, there is again a very violent fight over Freud. Maybe the particularity of post-post-modernity – with Deleuze, me, in some sense Slavoj Žižek, in France Quentin Meillassoux, and so on – is to return to these two references, and to completely assume that we are in discussion with Marxism and psychoanalysis, with Marx and Freud.

My philosophical framework, then, goes across four different sequences, four sequences which are very different, very opposed. And so, certainly, we are in the definition of philosophy given by Kant, because Kant said that philosophy is a battlefield. Across this context, across these four sequences, there are battles, there are victories, real victories and apparent victories, and there are returns, there are returns of ideas supposed defeated, dead. In philosophy we can absolutely say that there are ideas, thoughts, which we assumed are abolished, which disappeared, but which return, which rise again.

And so like my historical context, my philosophical context is a very vibrant battlefield. But my context also includes a very complex history of art, from the beginning of abstract painting to the modern from of deconstruction in the field of art, a complex history of music, transformations in the question of sexual difference, and sexuality as such, transformations in the questions of love, and so on and so on. During this span of time – this fifty, sixty years – there are very fundamental transformations in all fields, in philosophy, in politics, in history, in the arts, in concrete existence, and so on. And so, finally, this sequence of apparition and disparition is completely opposed to the conservative vision of the world as it is as a final and closed horizon. And so, I can say that maybe my vision cannot be exactly the same as that of today, that it cannot be exactly the same as that of a young man or woman today, *not because* the world is not the same, but more profoundly because my experience is not at all the experience of the continuity of a particular existence of the world, but fundamentally an experience of ruptures, of a sequence of ruptures.

Maybe my vision of the necessity of ruptures is only my biography, maybe this is my vision only because of the philosophical projection of my life.

If we cannot say that you live in a false world, if the world today is the true world, that is, if its really true that we are in a moment of history where the world as it is must continue, then it is also true that my experience, my personal experience during my life, is in contradiction with this world. And maybe my hypothesis, my philosophical vision of the world, is only a projection of my world, a projection of my experience, of my individual life, as a norm for the world as it is. If I desire a new possibility maybe its only because my life was a life with many sequences, many new emergences, many new possibilities, a life of catastrophic wars, of resistances and revolts, and so on and so on. And now we are progressively in the peaceful globalization of the world, we are in a world that is stable, a world which is a good world, and so on.

If all of this is true, then my first question – 'why as an old man I am speaking to much younger people' – was, in fact, a question of contradiction, of the contradiction between a vision of the world of my experience and this world of today. This other world was not the same as this world now, and it was not the same not only because of some little differences, but mostly because it was a world of change, a world of revolution, if you want, in all fields of humanity. It was a world of change and ruptures not only in politics, history and so on, but also in art, for example. And so it was not only a different world, but a world the fundamental law of which was different, it was a world under a very different law of the becoming of the world. Our situation in this class, then, is a dialectical one because there is a contradiction between two different, two absolutely different experience of the world as it is.

If our class is this sort of contradictory situation, then there are two distinct possibilities. The first possibility is that I transmit to you my experience – with some philosophical concepts, naturally – and after that you do what you want with this experience. And this is an interesting possibility, certainly. But it would transform our situation into something like a historical one, since all that would take place is the transmission of some historical experiences. In which case my duty is to transmit to you an experience of a world that was very different from your world, from the world of today. But there is a second possibility, which is that the relationship between us is not principally one of transmission, but rather an experience of the strange relationship between philosophy and time. There is a subtle but profound difference between the first possibility and the second.

The first possibility assumes that by the act of me telling you my experience – and especially my philosophical experience, the four sequences – all that can be achieved is the mere transmission of it to you, and so, that it is not possible to immediately produce any common consequences out of this contradiction. And so, the creation of a new common desire would not be possible. Finally, if I transmit to you my experience in this way, then I cannot know exactly what you will do with this experience. Naturally, this is because I cannot be on both sides. In this vision of the situation of the confrontation of my experience and your situation in the world today, the first possibility is reduced to one which is, in some sense, not a philosophical one, not only because it is historical in its very nature but much more because I cannot hope to directly create in you something like a new desire, a new desire which would be common to me and to you. And so we cannot hope to create a new community.

The second possibility is different. It is different because the point is that maybe the relationship between philosophy and time is *not* that sort of contradiction, and that it is *not* at all reducible to the contradiction between my experience and your experience. Naturally this difference is important and defines a sort of contradiction, but if philosophy, as apropos to time, is not reducible to the present, then it is possible that you and I could have some common use of this contradiction. It's a possibility, it's a possibility, *but only if philosophy is not reducible to the present.*

Certainly you recognize the conviction of the analytic vision here? Philosophy for the analytic position is absolutely reducible to the present, to the problems of the present. And this is why in the analytic tradition all that is really important are the papers of the last ten years – and the last ten years are the present. The conviction is that the only real problems and answers are those of the present, and that we must and can solve them. In the analytic vision, finally, the difference in time between two experiences cannot be useful for the present. And this is what we find in the analytic tradition the conviction that the history of philosophy – Plato, Descartes, Sartre, and so on – is too old... too old, too old to be useful. In this sense the analytic philosopher is exactly like the mathematician who says that Euclid is true and interesting, but finally of no value at all for modern mathematics. *If philosophy was in the analytic position, then we could not use the difference between the past and present in a common way in the present.*

You understand the problem? The point is to propose the idea that the relationship between philosophy and time is not absolutely reducible to the present of philosophy. We can say something like this: in philosophy the question is the question of the future, but as a question of the present posed from the point of view of the possibility of a new future, and the construction of this possibility is conditioned by a new transmission of the past. I repeat: the question of philosophy is the question of the possibility of a future *in the present*. The question of possibility is a very subtle question, because possibility is something that concerns the future but in some sense exists in the present – the future exists in the present in the form of possibility.

If philosophy is really something like this – if it is something which helps the existence of possibility in the present – then there is a construction of the future by means of a possibility, and I propose to say that in philosophy – specifically in philosophy – this construction of the future in the present is also a new transmission of the past. The consequence of this point is that the present of philosophy is also composed by the totality of its past – the present of philosophy is constructed by the totality of its past. But the philosophical thought of its own past is not a pure repetition, which would be a purely academic position, a reactive positions.

In France, for example, we know perfectly that the reduction of philosophy to the history of philosophy is the academic position, a purely academic position. But this is not what I am proposing here. My proposition is that the present of philosophy is the totality of its past *not by a repetition of the history of its past, but by the proposition of a new interpretation of its past...* or a part of its past. And why? Why must there be a new interpretation of the past in the present? For the construction of a future! It is for the construction of a future that is also a big future, and not a small future, but a future as big as the past! It is a future as big as the past because in the construction of this future there is a new interpretation of the past! And so there is a complete contemporaneity of philosophy to itself! *Plato is with us, now!* It is not something old, which is completely abolished. Its not dogmatists, existentialists and so on, and we have no use of all that. *Not at all! Philosophy exists precisely because Plato, Aristotle, Descartes and Kant and so on are with us, now*! Why are they with us now? Why? Because we can use of all of these old philosophers as a part of the construction of the future, as a part of the construction of the future by way of a new interpretation of the past. And so, in this future, which is in some sense a real and completely different future, there is also the presence of the totality of the philosophical past, because the new interpretation of Plato, for example, is a new interpretation *for* the future, in *this* future we have a new Plato. And this new Plato will be the new present of the future. It is only in philosophy that we have something like that... only in philosophy.

Naturally, maybe this is also a possibility in theatre, but that's another problem, and maybe I shall speak on this problem later.

And there is a very complex relationship between philosophy and theatre, a relationship that has existed from the very beginning. And you know why? Because in theatre too we can re-stage the past, we can re-stage Sophocles, Aeschylus, and so on, and so *they are with us*. But when we re-stage there is, naturally, a new interpretation precisely because we re-stage Sophocles in a different manner, in a different place than the Sophocles of the Greeks. And so, in theatre too we constantly have the possibility of a new interpretation of the past in the present *for the future ... for the future*. This difficulty is absolutely essential.

And so we have another contradiction because a part of the obscure position in philosophy is to say that philosophy, finally, is nothing else than the history of philosophy. This position studies Plato, Aristotle and so on, but in a strictly obscure manner, exactly like someone who desires the return of old religious forms of existence. *It's the same thing, it's the same thing...* it's the fetishization of the past. And this position is different from the analytic position, which states that all of the history of philosophy is closed, is finished, is of no interest, of no use for us. And *this* is the truly conservative position, and also the dominant position.

It is exactly the same contradiction that we had between the obscure position and the conservative position in politics, and so, to oppose it we have to use all of the past *in another manner*. We cannot repeat and we cannot return to the past, nor can we abolish this past. What we must do and what we can do is interpret this past in the light of the future.

What we must explain is how it is possible that the present of philosophy is also the interpretation of the past for the future. This is the second possibility of my speech here: an historical experience completely different than the world as it is today, transmitted in the form of a new interpretation, and somehow common to you and to me.... We can have the same future, you and me. And *if we can create a community*, it is, naturally, *because we can have this point is common*, which is the possibility of a new future somehow in the present. This is a very powerful idea: the unity of humanity is in the point of view of a future. Its a necessity – it is not only a philosophical symptom – that in philosophy we clearly see the past, all of the past, under a new interpretation as useful for the creation of a new future. But, finally, and more generally speaking, if you have the dream of a humanity, of generic humanity beyond the differences of sex, nationality, culture and so on, and of a generic humanity which respects these differences, and where these differences are inside this form of humanity, it is clear that this community *is from the point of view of the future*, because no matter how many differences there are between people they can have the same future, a future can unify them in their differences. *This is why philosophy is important*! *It is a sort of paradigm of all that*!

In philosophy it is clear that all of the past is with us. All of the past is with us because we can have a new future by means of a new interpretation of this past. And if all of that is true, then when I speak to you it is not only a transmission, a historical transmission, of an experience which is different from your experience, but a sort of experimentation of the philosophical possibility to transform the past into a future... to transform the past into a future. That is precisely the fundamental goal of philosophy, and it is also a clear answer to the reason for why you and me are in this room all together, together across the very important differences of historical experiences, philosophical experiences, artistic experiences, and so on between us. This answer is positive because it is not reducible to a pure exercise of transmission, which would be something interesting, certainly, but something very different than a philosophical experience.

And so we have our three concrete problems, and three generalizations of these concrete problems. Now, finally, I can propose our three subjects for the next few days:

First, the anthropological nature of philosophy: the relationship between philosophy and anthropological circumstances, or, if you want, philosophy as an exception, or even, the relationship between universality and particularity in philosophy, or, in another manner, the relationship between the universality of truth and the particularity of culture. Philosophy is a symptom of this very important problem today, which is the contradiction of the universality of truth and the particularity of culture. And we shall see that this relationship between universality and particularity is today the most important philosophical problem, and the most difficult. And second, the dialectical nature of philosophy: the dialectical nature of philosophy is the question of a rupture in philosophy, or, the question of philosophy as the thinking of ruptures and the relationship between continuity and ruptures. So it is the question of possibility, the question of possibility inside the world as it is. But more precisely the dialectical nature of philosophy is the question of what is in philosophy the fundamental contradiction and what is the goal of philosophy. We can say something like that for the moment, but what is more precise, naturally, is the idea that the fundamental contradiction in philosophy is a subjective one, and yet the goal is a common desire, not a common state or a common existence, but a common desire. And, finally, the paradoxical relationship between philosophy and time.

We have a good program in these three points, and we shall begin the treatment of this program tomorrow. Thank you to all of you.

2. Day Two

2.1 Lecture III

This afternoon we will return to the question of what I've named the anthropological nature of philosophy, that is, the relationship between the goal of philosophy, the goal of philosophical discourse, of philosophical references and so on, and the particularity of some culture, some country, some language and so on. In a very brutal form, the question can be: was there philosophy in old China? Or: was there philosophy in pre-colonial Africa? Or even: was there philosophy in Greece before Socrates, Plato and Aristotle? And so on. Generally that sort of question is objected to for the rational reason of the form: if you say that, for example, philosophy did not exist in old China, then you are saying that something was missing in that culture, and if you say that this thing which was missing in that culture is present in your culture, you are affirming the superiority of one culture over another. This is a very common argument against a proposition that asserts the non-existence of something in some culture. And you can all imagine what the progressive position is regarding such a proposition: it is precisely to find something like philosophy in old China, something like philosophy in pre-colonial Africa, and so on, because the idea of something missing, of something absolutely absent, in some culture is a sort of objection to that culture.

My answer is different: I think we can, absolutely, say no to that sort of question. I affirm that in old China there was no philosophy at all, and I will try to justify this point of view. Abstractly, we can say something like this: if you say that something is missing in a culture, all that you are saying is that there is a difference between one culture and another culture. And we can say that, generally speaking, if you establish a comparison between two cultures there is always something missing in one in comparison to the other, precisely because they are different. If everything that exists in one culture also exists in the other culture, then the two cultures are only variations of the same theme. And so, abstractly, there is no reason to identify the affirmation 'something is missing in some culture' with the affirmation 'something is inferior in this culture, in comparison to the other'... all we affirm by such a proposition is that something is missing, and, finally, that there is a difference between the two.

If you want to transform the affirmation 'something is missing in this culture' into an affirmation that proves the superiority of that culture over another, then you would have to give a proof not only that something is missing – in the second culture – but also that the presence of that sort of something is a proof of superiority. And this is a different argument, absolutely different. For example, we can absolutely affirm that many things are missing in our culture in comparison to many other cultures. I take one example: in many Indian cultures of North America we can find very extraordinary subjectivities in their myths. Levi-Strauss himself affirmed that to have myths with such subjectivities, and to have such references to the concrete situation of the collectivity and so on, is a sort of superiority of the Indian cultures over his own. We have, after all, no equivalent at all of something like that. And so, we can say that these sorts of mythologies, these sorts of stories concerning the destiny, the collective destiny of the people is missing in our culture. Okay! And it is so *by necessity*, if our culture is, in fact, different from the cultures of small Indian peoples in North America. This should not be surprising, after all, there is a difference between our culture and the cultures of Native

Americans. But we must also affirm that, naturally, something is missing in the Indian cultures in regard to ours. We can affirm, then, that the difference between cultures can always be expressed by the determination of something missing in one culture, something that is in the first culture and not in the second. I have no problem concerning this point.

Maybe we can find in countries and cultures where philosophy does not exist something else, *something else*. For example, we can find different forms of wisdom, traditional wisdom – which is very different from philosophy, but which is something really precious, and really unique. We can find different forms of morality, different representations of the relation to others, and so on. We can find, naturally, different forms of religious conviction concerning the destiny of life, different organizations of collectivity and so on. We can find different forms, *very different forms*, concerning the relationship to nature – its a very important question today, as you know – and we can find some cultures – some cultures which are disappearing because of our culture, which is an aggressive culture, a destructive culture, if you want – which have something really precious concerning the general vision of the relationship of humanity and nature, and so on and so on. And so, we must affirm that certainly something can be missing in other cultures, but in our culture too! And philosophy is something very particular. Of course, you could respond and say, 'okay, but philosophy must be universal'. Yes, philosophy must be universal... but every creation of a culture is, in principle, the possibility of a new universalism. Philosophy must be universal! But this is not an affirmation of concrete universality, and it is not an affirmation that a culture where philosophy does not exist is immediately a bad culture – there is, strictly speaking, no immediate relationship between two such affirmations.

We can affirm that philosophy, properly speaking, exists historically, and begins historically, in *particular* conditions and in *particular* cultures, without saying that this culture is superior to others on the basis of this fact alone. And why? Why does philosophy appear in its complete form in Greece, maybe five or six centuries before Christ? I think we can give reasons to this fact – it is a fact, and we can give reasons for this fact. I propose to say that there are five conditions for the existence of philosophy. And, finally, we must affirm that philosophy begins in Greece only because historically these five conditions were realized in Greece – *by chance, by chance*! It is not a miracle – the Greek miracle... – *but chance*! By chance these five things were together in Greece, and so the possibility, the birth of philosophy was realized. I want now to examine these five conditions.

First, I affirm that philosophy is a discourse, a proposition, concerning new propositions, new intellectual novelties concerning many questions. But there is a common point that is very important: philosophy accepts *as a law* the examination of all its propositions by others. If you want, philosophy is discussion. When the philosopher speaks, when the philosopher writes, he knows that all that he says and all that he writes will be discussed by others, by other philosophers and, finally, by everybody, everybody who freely reads the book, everybody who encounters the philosopher and so on. The philosopher *as such* is not the guarantee of the discourse, for the philosopher is not a king, he is not a priest, nor a prophet. It is not, therefore, the particularity or the absolute singularity of the position of the philosopher which is the guarantee of the discourse of the philosopher. The discourse of the philosopher is not a discourse from some sacred place of society. Maybe the philosopher says something true, but we would only know this by way of a discussion of what he has said, and not because the philosopher is a philosopher.

Naturally, some philosophers can use your... position, and transform this law of philosophy into something else. There is some effect of transference – in psychoanalytic language – there is some position of authority in play. This is always possible, but this is not in the very essence of philosophy. Philosophy is defined by discussion, and it is why the form of discussion is the appropriate form of philosophy in Plato. The dialogues in Plato are used precisely to give proofs – something like false proofs, proofs that are a little arranged, proofs that are of a theatrical nature, but they are proofs. And these dialogues are also proofs that philosophy is that which is exposed to discussion – all that is said in philosophy is exposed to discussion.

Philosophy, then, proposes a very different position on the question of the truth – truth as arrived at through discussion – than the conception of truth where the guarantee is the position of the one who speaks, be it a king, a priest, a prophet, or, finally, a God. Philosophy is, principally, the ambition to say the truth without the place of a God. The prophet, on the other hand, speaks because he is a sort of interpreter of God, and the king speaks because he has the power to speak, and, finally, the priest speaks because he is a religious representation, and so on, but the philosopher speaks only because he can produce arguments concerning what he says. And so we can say that philosophy is a free determination of thinking, a free determination of thinking from a social point of view.

Everybody can be a philosopher! It's not a fact, naturally, but it is a possibility, and this possibility is absolutely immanent to the definition of philosophy. Everybody can be a philosopher and everybody can discuss with the philosopher. And, again, we find this in the work of Plato: Socrates discusses with everybody, after all. And so, its really a free determination of thinking because the place, the social place of the philosopher is not prescribed by society, and the value of the discourse is not prescribed by the place of the philosopher in society, but only by the intrinsic value of the discourse. And this value is experimented by the discussion – not only by the discussion in that moment, but by discussions afterwards too, including new interpretations of that philosophy much, much later in the future. Everybody can speak – that is a right of the philosophic idea. And everybody can refute, everybody can refute.... And so, the first condition for the birth of philosophy is democracy, absolutely. But it is democracy in a very large sense: everybody can refute what is said by everyone else.

As you know – generally speaking – this is not the case in many other forms of society. In most societies it is not true that everybody can refute the king, or that everybody can refute the dictator, and so on. And certainly in many civilizations it's not true that everybody can refute the religious authority. If God is really the law of society, naturally, it cannot be the case that everyone can refute what He says. If God is God how could everybody refute Him? How could God's words, His authority be exposed to discussion – discussion by everyone? It is by definition that what God says is true, and so it is not exposed to discussion. The philosophical form of verification was, therefore, really something new, something very new. And so this first condition of philosophy was also a new conception of truth.

I insist on the point: philosophical truth – defined by the fact that it resists objections, resists refutations – is a new conception of truth. And this sort of negative definition of a truth is fundamental in philosophy. It is not an affirmative definition – it's true because God said it, it's true because the priest said it, because the king said it, and so on – it's a negative definition, because it is true *only if across discussions there is something which resists refutation – it is a proof, it is not an authority*. We must, then, understand that truth is not a fact but a result, a result of the experience of discussion. We can say, therefore, that in philosophy there is a collective dimension to truth, because it is a collective judgment across discussions and not a collective submission to power, including the power of God... if God speaks. We can image that God is mute, certainly, but generally, in the religious framework, God speaks, too much maybe.... In any case, there is something new, something different with philosophy. For example, even if a philosophy, or a philosopher, gives a proof of the existence of God – in classical metaphysics its practically always the case that the problem is to find proofs of the existence of God – even if a philosopher gives proofs of the existence of God, there is no consequence that this proof is the speech of God Himself. Such a proof – if such a proof is possible – is a proof by the rational means of philosophy itself, and so there is no immediate contradiction between the philosophical conviction that God exists and the fact that philosophy is a free determination of thinking. In such an instance, the philosopher proposes a proof of the existence of God, and after that the proof is discussed, exactly as a proof in mathematics. After all, we can always find somebody who says that some proof is not a proof, that the proof is not good, and so on. And so, finally, we can affirm that even the existence of God Himself can be in the field of free philosophical thinking – the existence of God is itself exposed to discussion, and not imposed by power or proved by revelation or some sacred book and so on.

We can, therefore, affirm that philosophy is defined by the lack of any sacred place or sacred book – it is only arguments, and free determination of thinking. Democracy – in the large sense of the term – therefore, is a condition for something like philosophy. Philosophy cannot appear, and certainly it cannot begin, in a context where the notion of truth is not completely detached from a form of power. The dependency of truth on power is an interdiction for philosophy. And so, I name democracy – not in the sense of the organization of the state with polls and so on, but in the more general sense of a disjunction between truth and power – the first condition for philosophy. In philosophy there is no relationship between truth and power, be it divine power or the power of a king. Philosophy can appear only in a democratic context – this is the first condition. And, as you know – politically speaking – democracy is a creation of the Greek society.

The second condition is not *this* freedom. This freedom of thinking, in fact, supposes – on the contrary – the existence of a common law of thinking. And so, while the first condition is a sort of freedom, the second condition – which is a condition for the possibility of argument, proof and the drawing of consequences – is not in the direction of freedom but in the direction of a law, a common law. After all, it is impossible to discuss a proposition without some law common to the philosopher and his interlocutor, some law concerning what is a discussion, some law concerning what is a rational discussion. Naturally, it is possible that someone responds to the philosopher merely by saying that what he says is not true, but if he merely say 'no, it is not true' and nothing else – if he does not give an argument – then it is not a discussion. And if there exists something like a discussion, then there must exist something like a common law of thinking appropriate to this discussion. And so, the possibility of a peaceful discussion – philosophy is not war, it is not civil war, after all – is the existence of common laws of thinking, common laws of regulating the discussion. And what is civil war, after all? Civil war is when we discuss power, when we discuss determination, without any common law. Naturally, in such a case we must fight, we must fight and we must be victorious. In philosophy it is the same: if there is no common conception of rationality we cannot have a true exposition of the philosophical proposition to a collective discussion.

And so, the absolute freedom of thinking – no sacred place, everybody can speak, everyone can question, and so on – is the first condition. But after that, the existence of philosophy requires that there exists the conviction that there is something like a common law, which is precisely rationality or logic, in a general sense. Therefore, we can say that discussion, rational discussion exists only if there exists a common logical framework, a common logic. And why? Precisely because argumentation is made out of the consequences of some proposition: you affirm something and after that you affirm something else, something that is a consequence of the first affirmation. And how do we pass from the first affirmation to the second as a consequence? It is possible only by something like a logical law, which is something like a proof or conviction that the second affirmation is the consequence of the first. Always, always there is something like this in the context of philosophy. If we propose to somebody to go from a first proposition (P1) to a second proposition (P2), there must be a rational passage, a rational transition, and we must suppose that the conception of rationality in this other person is common to ours. And so, it is an absolute necessity that there exists something like a common logical framework, a common law of rationality, in order for anyone to expose something to philosophical discussion.

There are, then, two very different conditions: the first one is freedom in thinking and the second is something like discipline, something like order, something rational, logical, not the power of a particular place but a rational common. These two first conditions, in fact, dispose something like a cultural framework: at the most elementary level freedom and logic, and their combination – absolute freedom, in some sense, and absolute logic, in another sense – are the axes of any culture. As you all know, when you read a philosophy you always find the two, you always find some combination of the two. For example, some philosopher may ultimately say that there is no limit, that there is absolute freedom, but, in fact, this is impossible because this freedom in the very exposition of itself to another must assume the idea of a common law. And so, a philosophy is always a very strange mixture between freedom and something like the absolute power of the law – not absolute power in the political sense, not absolute power like the power of the king, but an absolute power which is immanent, a power which is accepted by the freedom of thinking itself. If we do not have that sort of mixture, that sort of dialectical mixture between absolute freedom and absolute determination – determination within the framework of logic – we cannot have philosophical discourse, we cannot have philosophy.

The fact is that in Greece – for the first time in history – we have the idea of a proof. And the idea of a proof is a very specific idea: a proof is the idea that we can verify something as true purely by the strict consequences of a first affirmation – we have evidence of the first affirmation, *but we deduce* the consequences concerning the final destiny of that first affirmation. Minimally, that is the essence of a proof, of giving a proof. This is an invention, and it is an invention at a very specific place and time. In Greece proof was invented in the invention of demonstrative mathematics. We cannot say that the Greeks invented mathematics in general, because we find mathematics in other cultures – we find arithmetic, we find numbers, we find a sort of geometry, and so on. In fact, it has been demonstrated that even in some very small cultures there have been many mathematical manipulations, and so we cannot say that the birth of mathematics took place in Ancient Greece. But we can affirm that *there was the birth of demonstrative mathematics*, which is the idea that all mathematical propositions can be proved, that there is a proof for every mathematical sentence. And so, while the first condition of philosophy is democracy, the second is mathematics. The two are not at all the same – mathematics, after all, is not very democratic. In mathematics, in fact, it is often said 'you have to obey the law'. And this, certainly, is part of why mathematics is very difficult: mathematics is, in some sense, creativity, extraordinary creativity of thinking, but, in another sense, it is the sovereignty of the law, the absolute sovereignty of the logical law. This mixture is necessary, it is absolutely necessary for philosophy. And we find the two in Ancient Greece.

The third condition is the possibility of universality. Universality is the idea that all of that – affirmations, consequences, discussions, and so on – is addressed to everybody without restriction. There is a very important passage of Plato on this point: in *Meno,* Socrates wants to prove that everybody has the possibility to reach the fundamental ideas, and to give proof of this he speaks to a slave – because, in Ancient Greece, a slave is an example of someone who is, in some sense, outside of society, someone with whom the citizens have almost nothing in common. And so the discussion is a double proof: it is, certainly, a proof of a geometrical problem and so a proof of some truth, but the goal of the text is the proof that the slave is absolutely equal to everybody else, at least on the level of thinking as such. It is not an argument of political nature, because the conclusion of Socrates is not the abolition of slavery, or freedom for everybody, no, not at all. But it is a purely philosophical demonstration – a philosophical proof – and a concrete proof of absolute equality in the field of thinking. As we know, the slave is precisely the representation of humanity as such, he is the representation of the generic part of humanity, because the slave is without a particular place. Finally, there is nothing in common between Socrates and the slave, nothing except that both are human beings, and that both can think.

This was – *this is still* – a very fundamental moment in the history of philosophy precisely because it is an affirmation that rational discussion can be exposed to everybody, to everybody without any restriction – even to a slave. *That* is the universality of philosophy – and *Meno* is a concrete situation of this universality. The universality of philosophy is not reducible to the universality of its propositions, because it is also – and more profoundly in my opinion – the proposition that philosophy is addressed to everybody... philosophy is addressed to everybody.... Philosophy is for everybody, it is not only *formally* universal, *it is there for everybody*!

And so, there is in philosophy a fundamental idea of equality. In some sense, the first condition is liberty, but the third is equality. Obviously it is not the case that there was social equality in Ancient Greece – equality in this sense only came to exist as a possibility in the 19th century. There existed, however, the idea of equality in the field of thinking, and that is the philosophical sense of equality. The demonstration of Socrates is the philosophical affirmation and proof that the slave is equal in the discussion, in the philosophical discussion – there, at least, he is equal to everybody.

This philosophical equality is composed of two terms. The first is the concept of truth. But what is a truth, in fact? A truth is something that is not reducible to particularities, and so a truth is something that is for everybody, in the absolute sense. For example, it is the case that everyone is equal before a truth, everyone has access to truth, even a slave – and in the context of Plato the slave is the representation of humanity as such, because, after all, there is nothing to the slave which is like me, except that he too is a man and he too can think. Truth is the name of something – a proposition, or something else – which is for everybody in an absolute sense, which is for everybody without exception. The second term of this equality is that there exists something like human being in general, something which is not reducible to being a slave, being an aristocrat, being a rich man or a poor man, being Greek or barbarian, and so on. This something that is not reducible to any particularity, this something that is in every concrete human being, is the generic part of human being. The philosophical idea is that there is a generic part in every individual: in every individual, regardless of their culture, sex, age and so on, there is something which is an exception to particularity, which is that *this is a man, this is a woman. And this affirmation is universal by itself, it is universality itself.*

There is, therefore, in philosophy the recognition of the existence of something which is the generic part of human being in every individual, and a truth is something which is addressed precisely to this generic part. There are, consequently, no particular conditions required for understanding and accepting a truth – particularity, if it is a condition for access, a condition for the possibility of understanding, can only be in opposition to a truth. In principle, a truth is disposed to the generic part of a human being, to the generic part of every individual. A truth is in exception to all particularity. You see, then, that there is a relation between truth and its address? We can name this generic part the subject of human being, it is the human subject – it is a philosophical name. And so, we can affirm that philosophical universality is the composition of two fundamental concepts: truth and subject. We can find this idea under other names, more traditional names: subject can be the 'individual', or 'person', it can be 'consciousness', it can be many other names, and truth can be 'exception', 'transcendence', it too can be named by many names, many different names. The history of philosophy is, after all, a sequence of ruptures. But, finally, across the entire history we have the fundamental correlation between truth and subject, which is, finally, the correlation between what is universal and what is the subject of this universality. And this is why in the history of philosophy the question of truth and the question of subject are so fundamental – they are fundamental precisely because there is no philosophy without an understanding of what is equal in all human beings. And so universality is the third condition of philosophy.

But why is this a condition? Because very often in many cultures – and maybe in every culture – there has been, or there still is, a tendency to believe that a true human being is a human being of *that* culture, and that a human being of another culture is not exactly a human being. This is a very important fact in the entire history of humanity. For the Greeks themselves the question is somewhat obscure, because for the Ancient Greeks there were Greeks and barbarians, and so, maybe, a human being is first of all a Greek man. But philosophically this is not true. Philosophically we must affirm the idea of the equality of human beings in the field of thinking. And so, in philosophy there is something that is not reducible to any particular culture, something that is always, in some sense, beyond the laws of any proper culture. And, once more, we find this idea in Plato: philosophy is the corruption of young people.

Why is philosophy corruption? Precisely because in it there exists the idea that there is something which is more important than the law of a society, that there is something more important than the laws of any particular culture. This is not a negation of culture, and it's not a negation of particularities, but only the affirmation that something can be more important. As you probably know, this is the subject of the great play of Sophocles – *Antigone* – because the central idea of that play is that there exist laws that are beyond the laws of the city, beyond the laws of the country. And so, we can say that this play of Sophocles is, absolutely, a part of the conditions of philosophy, because it is an affirmation that there is something more important than the particularity of any culture, more important than the particularity of some political situation. And that something *is a new equality: it is an equality between human beings and not only between the citizens of some country*, it is an equality that affirms the absolute equality of all human beings as such, it is an equality between subjects, in the sense I give to the word. Philosophy is impossible without truth and subject – these two correlated ideas are a condition for the very possibility of philosophy.

The fourth condition... the fourth condition is related to the problem of language. And, naturally, it is related to the third condition – universality. We discussed this point yesterday: philosophy cannot affirm that it is in an exclusive relationship to one language, one particular language. And why? Because it would be a return to something that would not be philosophical under the first condition: if you affirmed that philosophy is by necessity in one language, and only in that language, then we would lose the complete freedom of thought – the complete exposition of a proposition to opposed judgments, to public judgment – which is constitutive of philosophy. In such a case philosophy would be something closed, something closed from the very beginning. If we want complete rational freedom of thinking we cannot affirm that philosophy must speak German, or Greek, or something like that. And so, when Heidegger writes that being speaks German – or Greek, for that matter – he is proposing something that is not philosophical. And so, at that moment, at the moment he proposes restricting philosophy to a single language *on ontological grounds,* he is not a philosopher, because he is proposing something that is outside philosophy, something that is not philosophy, and, in fact, something that is against philosophy.

Naturally, many philosophers from time to time say something that is outside of philosophy, something that is not philosophy, something that is non-philosophical or anti-philosophical – there is, after all, no guarantee that a philosopher always, or only, speaks philosophically. And so, a philosopher can certainly say something non-philosophical, he can propose some absurdity, some falsity and so on, and some aberration too. Philosophers, as we know, are precisely not kings, priests, prophets and so on, they are human beings and nothing else, and so they too can say something which is not at all in the genius of philosophy, something which is outside philosophy, something which is a position of nationalism, sectarianism, dogmatism, and so on. But, in principle, philosophy cannot admit any particular language as a sacred language, precisely because there does not exist a single language proper to philosophy, there does not exist a single particular language that would be the only possible language for philosophy. Such a language, if it existed would – regardless of which language it is – be a sacred language, and philosophy is that which does not have a sacred language.

But there is another question: if the language of philosophy cannot be German, Greek, etc., then, finally, what is the composition of philosophical language? What is the language of philosophy, finally? The answer to this question is strange. In one sense philosophical language is rational: it is discussion, arguments, consistency of the discourse, proofs, and so on. In this sense philosophical language is very near mathematical language. This proximity is, as you all know, evident across the history of philosophy. The *Ethics* of Spinoza, for example, is written as such: it is proposition, definition, axiom, principle and so on, it is written in – and this is its classical name – geometrical form. You find something like that also in the *Tractatus* of Wittgenstein, and we find something like that in the logical work of Aristotle too. Across the entire history of philosophy we have the possibility that philosophical language is a formal language, in some sense, or at least that it is near formal language. But across this same history we also find the contrary possibility: we find the possibility that philosophy is written in the language of poetry. We find this, for example, is Lucretius, but also in Plato – the great myths and so on, which are absolutely of poetical nature, with images, metaphors, inventions, and so on. Philosophical language – even if we just look at the history – is between two possibilities: the mathematical possibility, which is a formal language, and, on the other side, poetic language, with images, metaphors and so on. If we read Nietzsche, for example, we find poems, we find images, we find something which is very close to prophesy, but when we read Spinoza we have the contrary, we have mathematical form. This is strange, after all... it is strange....

Why is philosophy possible in such different languages? And we cannot propose a choice between the two – this is absolutely impossible! And, in fact, we have this mixture form the very beginning! In Plato, for example, we find long sequences of pure argumentation, precise discussions of words, definitions and so on, and then we find the contrary, we find some strange stories from non-existent countries, we find strange myths, obscure visions and so on. From the very beginning and across the entire history of philosophy we find this fundamental impurity of philosophical language. There is no pure philosophical language – *it does not exist*.

We can say what is pure mathematics: it is when mathematics is written in – practically – a pure formal language. And we can also say what is pure poetry: when the poem is clearly written in a poetical style, with verses, and so on. But we cannot define philosophical language. In fact, we can absolutely affirm that there is no philosophical language. And this is a difficulty... it is a real difficulty. In consequence, and as a condition of the existence of philosophy, we must admit a language that is absolutely impure, a language which is neither mathematics nor poetry, but both. And, as you all know, it is this impurity that is so often the cause of the great difficulty of reading philosophy. Why? Because philosophy can pass from absolute and terrible abstraction, to very concrete considerations of examples, to,

finally, poetry. For example, in Hegel's *Phenomenology of Spirit*
– which is a very, very difficult text – the last words are a poetic
citation – in *Hegel there is a poetic citation at the end*! And in
this book of Hegel, in this great book of philosophy, we pass
from references to theatre and discussions of mathematics, to the
history of philosophy, to Schiller, and so on – it is a complete
impurity!

And, finally, why is such a situation a condition of philosophy?
Because we must accept that language can be absolutely impure.
In society, in general, there is a classification of different sorts of
languages – poetry, mathematics, politics and so on – but in
philosophy we must accept that all languages are possible. And
so the invention of philosophy is also the invention of something
that is beyond the normal forms of languages, beyond the
normal classification of languages and differences between
languages. In philosophy we can go from mathematics to poetry
– and this is absolutely paradoxical! In philosophy all the forms
are possible. And, finally, there is something inside of this
impurity of language that is real a communication, a real
transmission.

In some cultures it is impossible to do this, it is impossible to
have the mixture of different languages, and so it is impossible
to have philosophical language. This is the case in some
civilizations, in some great civilization, where it is precisely the
classification of languages which is most important, the most
important law – the language of the prophet cannot be the
language of the ordinary life, it cannot be the language of the
poet, or of the priest, and so on.

There is, therefore, something of philosophy that is opposed to
classification. This is an important idea: philosophy is against
classification, in particular against the classification of
languages, and it is why there has been for a long time a
contradiction between philosophy and the university, between

philosophy and academic discourse. As you know, I am a professor – I affirm this absolutely – and there are many philosophers in the university. And so, it's not an empirical contradiction, but it is a fundamental contradiction. And why? Because the discourse of the university – to speak as Lacan – is a discourse where classification is something that is very important. In the university, as you all know, there is classification: there is science and there is literature, and so on, and then there is more classification, for example, within history you have histories of certain types, modern history, contemporary history, history of this, history of that, and so on. And this is the genius of the university: its genius is precisely the continuous invention of new classifications, new specializations, its genius is the establishment of ever more specific particularizations. Even science, finally, is decomposed into many parts, and so you have cellular biology, zoology of insects, and so on and so on. And then you constantly have the choice of something, the choice of a language, and the choice of some part of a language.

There is, of course, a fight against this particularization within the university itself: interdisciplinary studies, mixtures between different specialties, and so on and so on. And all that is, in fact, a fight against the genius of the university itself. It's a fight against the university from inside the university – something like that. But it is also why this fight is always a failure. Why? Because even with the combinations of fields and with interdisciplinary studies we return, slowly but eventually, to ever further classification. Why? Because it is the law, it is the law of the university, and it is the law of the world today.

The origin of the discourse of the university, however, is from inside of philosophy, in fact. The invention of classification – in the sense of classification within the university – was an invention of Aristotle. In fact, we can say that Aristotle is really the man because of whom there exists the possibility of academic philosophy. Why? Because inside of the philosophy of Aristotle classification is absolutely fundamental. This was, in fact, the genius of Aristotle and it was he who created the discourse of the university. Undoubtedly Aristotle was the first great professor! Plato is not a professor – nobody in the dialogues says, definitively, what Plato is thinking. What is Plato's final thought? Where is it? We cannot find it! It is never definitively stated, but is always a sort of vague circulation of discussion. And who is Plato, after all? In all the books of Plato there is Socrates. In Plato it is always something or someone else who speaks – a stranger, Socrates, Thrasymachus, Protagoras, and so on. It's a theatre, a theatre! And so we have the theatre of Plato and the university of Aristotle, at the very beginning of philosophy – it's a form of the impurity of language, after all.

But to accept this language without closure, this impurity of language, we must accept to go beyond classification, which is also to go beyond the university. And so there is always a tension between philosophy and the university – sometimes inside the university itself. For the true philosopher the academic discourse is not completely adequate. The university is adequate only for the analytic position, but there, naturally, you accept classification!

In Greece we have the creation of the possibility of the impurity of language, and the creation of a language that is completely impure. In fact, in some sense, in Ancient Greece we have the invention of all of the possibilities of philosophical language – from poetry to mathematics. We have great philosophical poems in Greece – Parmenides, for example, was a poet, and Heraclitus too – but we also have the language of the university, in Aristotle – definition, classification, and so on – and even in Plato we have – in some passages – a language of philosophy which very near mathematics. In Plato we have mathematization

but we also have myths, stories, metaphors, images, and so on –
in Plato we have it all! It's a theatre, it's really a theatre! And so,
in Ancient Greece we do not find the invention of *the language
of philosophy*, but precisely *the in-existence of the language of
philosophy*. And to invent something which does not exist is
very difficult.... For example, the invention of God....

The invention of God is something very extraordinary because
to invent something that – probably – does not exist is a true
creation! And, as you know, in theological discourse it is said
that this is how God created the world – he created it from
nothing. And so, pure creation is creation from nothing! But – I
propose – that a great example, maybe the greatest example, of
creation from nothing is God himself – He is really created from
nothing! It is much more God who was created from nothing
than the world by God. Why? Because if there is God – God is
not really, but... – if there is God, there is no problem: God is
without limit by definition, and so we can perfectly accept that
He could create something out of nothing – we cannot impose
limits on God, after all, we cannot limit him to creating
something only from something else, God is pure potency, and
so God can create the world from nothing, it's not a problem.
But how can we, how can human beings create something from
nothing? It's much more difficult, certainly. But it is possible,
and I think that God himself is a perfect example.... And *God is
a creation*! He's really a creation, a creation from nothing! But
he is a negative creation, finally, because there is nothing in the
world which could have been an example, nothing that could
have been the material, the substance for the creation of
something like God – everything in the world is finite and God
is infinite, everything in the world has limits and God has no
limits, and so on. And so, He is a negative creation, and a
creation that absolutely proves the genius of human being, which
is the capacity of man to create something out of nothing. After

that, if God creates something from nothing it is really not so surprising.

You must understand that the point is that philosophy demands that we accept a language that is absolutely impure – the language of philosophy cuts across all languages, from poetry to mathematics – and, finally, a language that in-exists. Philosophy accepts a language that is not a language, because, finally, there is no language of philosophy. With philosophy the old Greeks invented something the language of which does not exist as a specific form of language, they invented something the possibility of which is to go across all forms of language – the juridical form, the mathematical form, the poetical form, and so on. And, as I have said, you find this impurity across the entirety of philosophy's history. At the time of Plato and Aristotle all the possible forms of language existed, and *as a consequence* philosophy became a possibility.

In fact we can even say that this creation is, in some sense, homologous to the creation of God, because it is really a creation from nothing and the creation of something that does not exactly exist. We could ask, for example: what is the possibility of a language that is not reducible to any particular existent language, to any real language? And this impurity is the source of both the difficulty of philosophy and the strength of philosophy. It is the source of difficulty because it is difficult to go across such different languages. I am aware of this problem because, as you know, I go from pure mathematics and poetry – I go across all the different languages. The difficulty is not the use of a particular language, but the passage from one language to another, the difficulty is to move across such different languages and yet create something unified. This unity, this unification, is the great difficulty of a philosophical construction, certainly. And, in fact, it is not so much the conceptual construction itself that is difficult, the difficulty really is within the question of language, because we have to say something in one language and something else in another language, and we must pass from the first to the second.

The last condition is the question of the transmission of philosophy. The problem of philosophy is that *philosophy is not reducible to written texts*... and the transmission of philosophy is not reducible to the written. There has always been what I name physical transmission, that is, transmission with the body of the philosopher... like here, finally: there is the body of the philosopher, the voice of the philosopher, the presence of the philosopher, and so on. From the very beginning philosophy exists not only in the form of texts – written texts, books and so on – but always also in the presence of the philosopher – the voice, the body and the physical existence of the philosopher. And, finally, this is why there exists something like an effect of a philosopher and a philosophy: in the transmission of philosophy there is something like transference, something like love, in fact – if love is something that requires the presence of the other, its physical presence. Naturally, you could object and say 'but you are also a professor of mathematics'.... but *it is not the same*, it is not the same.... And why? Because the potency of mathematics, of the transmission of mathematics, is mathematics itself, absolutely. Certainly, there are good professors and bad professors in mathematics, but this is not the point. With philosophy – and with the transmission of philosophy – we cannot separate it from the philosopher. In philosophy we have proper names – Plato, Aristotle, Heidegger, Sartre, Deleuze and so on – and they are important, absolutely. And in this sense philosophy is like art, like poetry – with Mallarme, Stevens, Valery, Celan, and so on – and precisely not like science. In science there exist, naturally, the proper names of the scientists, but they are not at all important, what is important is the names of the theorems. In philosophy you cannot escape the proper names: if we speak of Plato we speak of Plato.

The transmission of philosophy is not purely rational, and it cannot be purely rational... *the transmission cannot be purely rational*! Why? Why? Precisely because the transmission of philosophy includes the philosopher! The ideal of philosophy is, certainly, rational – the philosopher is not a king, or a priest, or a God, and so what is said is exposed to discussion, and what is said is true only through discussion, through argument, through proof – but the transmission of all that, and so the very cause of entering into philosophy, into a philosophy, is not completely reducible to the rational discourse, because of this surplus element in the transmission, and in the discussion, which is the presence of the philosopher, his voice, and so on.

Certainly the most paradoxical case concerning the presence of the philosopher is Derrida. The work of Derrida is – at least in part – a polemic against presence and for writing, and so it is a polemic for the written against the voice. There are, Derrida has said, illusions of presence in the voice, in the physical expression, and so true transmission is writing. But Derrida was constantly present, he was more present than any other philosopher... *he was everywhere*! He spoke for hours and hours and hours and hours... and, finally, the oral work of Derrida is much more important than his written work. I don't say this against him, *not at all*... I say it only as a proof, a proof that we cannot escape the fact of the physical existence of the philosopher. And this fact is why after the death of some philosopher something continues.

In Ancient Greece, in fact, immediately after the Greek sequence of philosophy there were many books on the lives of the great philosophers – it was, practically, a new genre of literature in Greece. And these books, very often, were novels, pure inventions, but they were inventions concerning precisely the physical presence of the philosophers, the lives of the philosophers. And, of course, we still have this today. And it is a symptom of this surplus. It is a symptom of the idea that something was said by the philosopher, but is not in the books, that the philosopher said something and that *this something* is the real key, the real secret of the philosopher. But why does all of this exist? Because there really is something in the transmission of philosophy – something *necessary for the transmission of philosophy* – which cannot be purely rational, something which is somehow effective, somehow material, physical, something like love for another.

And why? Because at the core of philosophy is a subjective transformation... and it is as rational as possible. There is, at the core of philosophy, a rational transformation, but a rational transformation by means that are not completely rational, which cannot be completely rational. And again, why? Because subjectivity *as such* is not purely rational, is not reducible to something purely rational – the rational, the universal, are a part of human being, but not the totality. And so, naturally, if you want a subjective transformation, there is a part of that transformation which is not reducible to rational arguments.

Finally, philosophy – the goal of which is not only rational conviction, but a new desire – also must have a presence, and not only the presence of a book. *Philosophy is not reducible to books*! Philosophy is not reducible to books.... Books are important, absolutely, *but even books are not reducible to books*! To read a book of philosophy is not reducible to the arguments of the book. There must be love... there must be something of love at the very beginning of philosophy. There is some presence there, maybe, something like a spiritual presence. Okay, we stop.

2.2 Lecture IV

I have supposed a geographical, historical and human place
where, *by chance*, the five conditions of philosophy existed: we
had in this place the form of democracy – not real political
democracy – and so the possibility of free discussion, we had
mathematics, and so the possibility of a proof, we had also the
possibility of the impurity of languages, a sense of universality –
not in the political sense, but in the sense that there is something
in every human being which is its generic part, and that
philosophy is addressed to this part of every subject, and so, that
truth is beyond every particularity – and, finally, we had the
philosopher, his presence. All that existed in a place, a small
place, in fact, and for a short time. The existence of philosophy
is a possibility, and this possibility was for the first time realized
in a small part of the Greek empire. This small place, naturally,
was Athens, and this short time was three or four centuries –
which is not a great time – with two fundamental centuries,
before the birth of Christ. And this is really the beginning of
what we can name philosophy properly.

Naturally, we can name philosophy some other things: it's a
possibility, for example, to name philosophy some Oriental
wisdom, or some Native American mythologies, and so on. But
if we take philosophy in a limited and precise sense, then it came
to existence in a small place and short time – and in this place
and at this time philosophy was born. And after this there is no
real continuity of philosophy, but only something like a series of
great historical moments of the existence of philosophy.
Between these moments of philosophy's existence there has

been something else, something we can name analytic philosophy or scholasticism.

I name scholasticism precisely the idea that philosophy is a set of good problems and good answers. And there is something like that during the entirety of the Medieval sequence, and there is something like that today with analytic philosophy. Analytic philosophy is clearly scholastic. And scholasticism is something, it is not nothing at all: scholasticism is really something which exists, something which proposes some problems, studies some histories and some ideas, and, finally, some answers too, and so on. I only wish to say that, for me, it is not philosophy proper, but something else, something else... something which comes from philosophy but which is not exactly philosophy because it is a reduction of philosophy to the discourse of the university. *It is not philosophy...* but it is not nothing. And scholasticism, in the positive sense, is a good name: it is a set of problems and answers, collectively discussed, within the world as it is, and in some closed place – during the Medieval sequence it was in the monastery, and it was an activity of religious people, and today it is an activity in the university, in the closure of the university. There are, in fact, many similarities between scholasticism during the in the Medieval sequence and analytic philosophy in the university today.

We have academic philosophy every time that there is something homologous to the misunderstanding of Greek philosophy during the Roman Empire. It's the same case, always! In each case there is something which has the appearance of philosophy but which is not really philosophy. And why? Precisely because the conditions, the true conditions of philosophy, are absent, are lacking. As you know, for example, during the sequence of the Roman Empire there is practically no mathematics at all. There was democracy – not in the political sense, but in the sense of the possibility of free discussion – but it was quickly destroyed. In all, during this time the conditions of philosophy were not there, and so philosophy was not there! But, and maybe more importantly, there was a sort of repetition of Greek philosophy but without a true understanding the genius of philosophy itself. It is very interesting, for example, to read the Roman translations of some books of Greek philosophy – for example Cicero's translations of Plato – because, if you read them, you will not recognize the translations, the translations are something else, something very much outside of the significance of Greek philosophy.

The history of philosophy, then, is made of ruptures, of discontinuities – there is no continuity but only great historical moments of the history of philosophy. For example, we have the great metaphysicians of the 17th century: Descartes, Malebranche, Spinoza, Leibniz. This century was certainly a century of great philosophical creation, and the central concept of this sort of metaphysics was God. Certainly it was not a homologous century, philosophically – there were many differences, many disagreements and so on, and, finally, many different but essential proofs of His existence – but, the central concept was God, and the central problem was His existence. But this God, as Quentin Meillassoux has explained – this God of 17th century metaphysics – was not at all the religious God. In fact, at this time there was something like a transformation of the religious God into something else, into, precisely, the metaphysical God and the two are absolutely not the same. Naturally the metaphysicians claimed that it was the same God – they could not say that it was not at all the same God, that was, of course, too dangerous – but they are not at all the same, the metaphysical God is not the religious God. And so, when Pascal said that the God of Descartes is not the true God, he was right – it's true, the God of Descartes was not the religious God, and It was not Pascal's God, certainly not. The God of Pascal was, really, the Christian God, and the God of Descartes was an abstraction, a mathematical abstraction. This is why Descartes can give a proof of God's existence. The existence of the Christian God, the religious God, cannot be proved, because it is a revelation... it's a revelation... Christ, the Father and the Son and so on, we cannot have a demonstration of all that, it's not possible.

The 17th century – the century of the great metaphysicians – is the creation of the conceptual vision of monotheism, of the vision of God as a concept, of the transformation of God from an existence to a concept, and it is why we have a return to existence by proof. But if you must give a proof of the existence of God you are not in religion, naturally. In religion there is something else first, which is precisely the existence of God and not the existence of the concept of God. With existence by proof we are in philosophy, we are really in philosophy: it's not the God of religion, it's not the sacred God, it's not the God who speaks, it's really a philosophical construction, a human construction, by the means of rational concepts which propose a definition of God, and, after that, a proof of the existence of God, no different then the construction of a mathematical proof. The God of 17th century metaphysics is, finally, a mathematical God! This is the case for Descartes, it's the case for Leibniz, and it's the case for Spinoza. The case for Malebranche is more complex, because... – Malebranche is an extraordinary thinker – because Malebranche wanted to prove the Christian God, he wanted to give a proof of the existence of the Christian God, of the necessity of the Redemption by Christ and so on. Malebranche is a baroque philosopher because the goal of Malebranche is to transform Christianity itself into a philosophy, and not to efface, not to injure, but to make it into a philosophy. It's a complete failure, naturally, but it's interesting, *very interesting*. This was the first great moment of the history of philosophy.

The second great moment of philosophy – after Ancient Greece and the 17th century – is German Idealism, with Kant, Hegel, Fichte, and Schelling. This time the most important concept is the subject. We have moved from God to the subject – and this, in fact, was the great revolution of Kant. Later, Kant too would return to God, but He was in a secondary position. For Kant the most important concept is the subject, absolutely, and it's the same across all of German Idealism at the beginning of the 19th century.

After this there is the very international moment before the First World War. At its beginning – at the end of the 19th century – is Nietzsche, but after that we have Husserl in Germany, Bergson in France, Russell in England and so on. This moment too is very interesting, very creative, but also very international. And, on the whole, we can say that the most important concept of this moment is life. And so we have – across these moments – a movement from God, to subject, to life.

And, finally – this is, naturally, not the complete history of philosophy, but only a sequence of its greatest moments – we have what I name the French moment of the second part of the last century. This moment extends – if you permit me another narcissistic example – from Sartre to me. Over its course we have Sartre, Merleau-Ponty, Lacan, Althusser, Foucault, Lyotard, Derrida, Deleuze, Ranciere, and so on, for example, me. And in this moment – I think – we have an attempt to construct a philosophy with structure, subject and life – but without God, without God.... And, certainly, the most difficult problem of this sequence is to realize some synthesis between structure and subject... between structure and subject, yes, something like that.... The idea is that there is something subjective, something not completely reducible to structure, and the task is to define how in this small interval something like freedom is possible. Naturally, if the subject is purely reducible to structure, then we have no place for freedom. In the philosophy of consciousness – like in Sartre, for example – we have no place for freedom because *the subject itself is freedom*. On the other hand, if the subject is a structure – like it clearly is across practically all of this sequence – then there is no clear place for freedom. And so, the place of freedom is just between subject and structure.

All of these examples – across their differences – show us that the fundamental problem of philosophy is universality. We can even say that *philosophy is universal by itself*! The goal of philosophy is to open the possibility of something universal, of something that is really for every subject. And, as we have seen, the relation between truth and subject is precisely the attempt to realize that sort of universal proposition. But this process – the construction of this universality – is always situated, completely situated in a concrete world, in a space and time. These constructions are not only situated in concrete worlds very different from one another, but they are – generally – very short sequences in history, they are not at all some great permanent constructions, which continue indefinitely. They are moments, only moments of history. And why? Because this universality is conditioned – there are conditions for the possibility of philosophy – and so philosophy has the possibility of coming into existence only in very specific conditions of place and time. And so we must ask: how is something like that possible? Or: how we can explain that something universal is precisely inside some very particular conditions?

As you know that there is today a judgment that, finally, philosophy is something like an ideology of the western world, from Greece to today – from Greece to the United States – and not at all a universal disposition of humanity as such. The argument is simple: how can we speak of universality when it is clear that the creation, development and existence of philosophy is absolutely linked to small places and short times in the general history of humanity? And if we say that there is no philosophy in old China, no philosophy in pre-colonial Africa, and so on, and maybe that, finally, the places of philosophy have only been Greece, France, Germany – three small countries in the world as such – how we can we maintain the idea that philosophy is really of universal in nature? It's a great problem. And what is the philosophical translation of this problem? It's an empirical argument, after all, that the process of philosophy is linked to very particular conditions. There are two possibilities.

The first possibility is to maintain that philosophy, in fact, exists as something particular and is a part of our situation – you can be absolutely relativist, its a possibility. And to the question 'what is philosophy' you would then give the answer: philosophy is a part of the ideological existence of the western world and nothing else. It is a possibility, certainly. And if you are a relativist you could maintain that all that exists are cultures, that all that exists is particularity, and so you could ask: why would philosophy be an exception to that? The first possibility is precisely to maintain that philosophy is not an exception, that philosophy cannot pretend to be an exception, that there is no exception... that everything of intellectual nature, all ideas, in fact, are ideological, that they are all relative, particular, and so on. Finally, the first possibility is to say that philosophy cannot escape the judgment that everything is explained by particularity, and, naturally, that everything pertains only to cultural particularities. This is the first possibility.

The second possibility is to conceptually transform the problem and to explain – to propose, in fact – a new conception of universality and truth. After this, you would then have to explain how it is that even if a truth is constructed within a very specific context, this is not, by itself, an objection to the universality of that truth. And so, the second possibility demands that you explain not only how the conception of the universality of truth is possible in spite the particularity of its existence, but how it's possible from within the particularity of its existence. For this solution we have to propose – philosophically – that the idea of universality, or more generally a truth, is by necessity in relationship with a theory of the concrete world, in which that sort of truth is constructed or appears, but is irreducible to it. And this, in essence, is precisely my problem: my philosophical problem is to solve the question of truth, universality and so on, without the easy solution of pure relativism, which consists in the suppression of the problem. The relativist solution is the easy solution – we simply suppress the problem – and the other possibility is, certainly, more difficult.

I have attempted to solve this problem by a *complete transformation* of the relationship between universality and particularity. My first affirmation is to affirm that all that exists is particularity, and so a truth – if something like truth exists – is in a particular world and is constructed with particular material. Mathematical truths, for example, appear in Greece for very material and explicit reasons, and there is a relationship, an explicit relationship, between the universality of mathematics and the process of the construction of mathematics in Greece. We must admit this, but we must also affirm and prove that this particular process can have some results which are beyond the process itself, results which can be understood from a completely different point of view, from another world, in fact. There are many example of this: for instance, the demonstrations of Euclid can be understood today, even though we are in a completely different context than Euclid – we can read his demonstrations, and we can understand that they are proofs, and, finally, *we agree with these proofs*, with the result of these proofs. And how? How is this possible, if it was written by some Greek many centuries ago? Our task, then, is to explain this strange fact: we must explain how it's possible that something has been written, produced, understood and so on, in a completely concrete context without being reduced to the context.

The concept that I propose is immanent exception: in some circumstances, under some concrete and particular conditions, it is possible that a completely concrete process in a determinate world produces a result which, in part, is not reducible to the context and the process itself, and which is, in some sense, an exception to this context, to the laws of this context. But it's not an exception in the sense of the difference between God and nature, or an exception in the sense of the difference between the intelligible world and the sensible world, like in Plato – first in Plato, but after that as well – no, its an immanent exception: all the material of the construction of a truth is inside the particular world, but the result – which, materially, is absolutely of this world – is some new truth which can be understood from another word, from a world which is completely different. And so this exception is not an exception that comes from outside, but an immanent exception concerning something inside the world itself.

We must understand that a truth is situated, that *it is not in another world* – a truth is not God... it is not something from some other divine world. A truth is a construction, a human construction, truth is a human construction – there is no other world but the world of humanity. But this human construction can be understood from another point... not always, but it is a possibility – *universality is a possibility*. We return to our beginning: universality is a possibility, it is the possibility of being understood from another world, and not only in the world of its construction.

During long sequences nobody understands a truth. It's a fact, for example, for the last inventions in the mathematical field by Archimedes: during many centuries nobody understood anything of what he meant, and then, finally, at the end of the 16th century, there is an understanding of that sort of truth – it was absolutely obscure during many centuries. And so, we have something like a resurrection of a truth: the truth was dead, in some sense, it was reduced to the context of its birth and it was dead, but it can be resurrected, and this resurrection is its universality. Universality, finally, is the constant possibility that *if* something is a truth, then there can be a resurrection of this truth in another world. And it's not miracle, but precisely a change of circumstances, and with new circumstances that sort of truth can finally be understood again.

All that must be explained, but first I can give some examples of what I name a truth – they are only examples – because you must first be able to recognize the nature of that sort of exception. The examples, naturally, are very arbitrary. For example, new forms of thinking war and strategy in old China – I commence with old China because I have said that there was no philosophy in old China, and so, I want to absolutely affirm that there were some truths in old China. We must recognize that there is no symmetry here: we can have truths without philosophy, but it is impossible to have philosophy without first having some truths. In fact this is the more common situation – we have truths but no philosophy – because philosophy is precisely the construction of the concept of Truth out of artistic truths, political truths, scientific truths, and so on. And so we can also absolutely confirm that truths are a problem and construction of art, science, politics, and so on, and not of philosophy – whose construction is Truth. With Sun Tzu, certainly, there was the creation – within the context of old China – of a conception of strategy and the thinking of war which is absolutely of universal nature, because we have something like that in Clausewitz – another great thinker of war – and after that Mao Zedong and so on. And *we know, we can absolutely confirm,* that Sun Tzu's conceptions – explained many, many centuries before us – of what is a strategy, and, in fact, of what is a defensive strategy in war – and the strength of defensive war – is a truth from within a completely different world than his. Another example is mathematics in Greece: geometry and arithmetic. Another is the new form of love proposed in Medieval Japan. The testimony of this is the extraordinary novel *The Tale of Genji* – probably the most beautiful novel ever written concerning the question of love. It's extraordinary. And it is a novel of a woman – Murasaki Shikibu – *in Medieval Japan*. And this book, in fact, is a proof not only of the creation of an amorous truth in Japan, but also a proof of an artistic creation – the novel – in Japan many, many years before its resurrection in the western world. This book is as profound, as sublime, and as beautiful as Proust – there is, in fact, something near Proust in the novel of Murasaki Shikibu. Another example is the new physics in Italy with Galileo Galilei. Another is the new forms of sculpture in pre-colonial Africa. As you know, there has been a resurrection of African sculpture in the field of modern art. In fact, sculpture after Picasso, is completely fascinated by African sculpture, which is the creation of many centuries ago, and in a world which was completely different than ours. And so, this resurrection of pre-colonial African sculpture is a very powerful example of what is a resurrection: the context of contemporary art, in France, in Spain, in the United States, after – during and after – the First World War is completely different than the world where these great African sculptures were made centuries before colonization, and yet a great part of contemporary sculpture is directly a resurrection of pre-colonial African sculpture. There is also the new form of cinema in the United States, before and just after the First World War, with Chaplin, Griffith, and so on. Another example is contemporary new music in Austria at the end of the 19th century, with Schoenberg, Webern and Berg and so on. New painting in France at the end of the 19th century too, with Cezanne, Picasso and Braque. There are many more examples, but we will stop here.

All of these are what I name truths: they are all exceptions to reducibility to context, they are all creations which give the possibility of resurrection in another world. Naturally – and this we all know very well – the great majority of, for example, artistic creations disappear and cannot be truly resurrected. But there exist exceptions, which are universal precisely because it is possible that one day, in some other world completely different, and sometimes many, many centuries later, we can have an understanding, a completely new understanding – because we would be in a different context, a different world – of this creation, and we can continue this creation. This is the history of universality. Universality is not at all a matter of general propositions or something like that, it is not a question of abstraction. Universality is creation, human creation, it is human creation and human resurrection not of something general, but of something singular. Universality is the character of some creation that comes to constitute a part of the history of humanity. If I can use a technical term: it is a question of subtraction and not abstraction.

That sort of universality exists, its not a problem – we do not have to discuss that fact, the fact exists. We have many, many examples of something like that – intellectual creations, artistic and political creations, which have the strength, the possible strength to be exposed to resurrection – and so we can say that the universality of truth, the possible universality of what I name truth, is not a possibility but a fact. The question of truth, in fact – and this is my conviction – is not an abstract question, but an empirical one.

The most impressive fact is, certainly, the paintings found in the Chauvet-Pont-d'Arc cave, in France: these paintings are thirty-thousand years old, and they are magnificent paintings, and they can be compared... and yet we find the resurrection of this ancient paintings in Picasso. I gave this example at the beginning of my book – *Logics of Worlds* – because it's something truly fascinating. We cannot imagine what the life of man was thirty-thousand years before us – it's complete speculation, we can know very little about it – and yet we see this painting and we have an emotion, an effect, an understanding of all that – of the beauty, the strength, the signification of that sort of painting – and that, finally, is a proof of the existence of human being, not of cultures, but of the generic part of cultures. Maybe even our understanding is not the same as those men and women – of whose lives we can know nothing – but there are these paintings, and there is resurrection, and we affirm it the moment we see the paintings. I affirm that the existence of creativity, of truths, by humanity *is a fact, and not a speculation* – it is not a pure and abstract possibility, but a fact.

Philosophy comes after. But philosophy *must affirm* that the fact of the universality of truths is rational – philosophy must explain this fact, it must be exposed, this is a task of philosophy. The task of philosophy is not to create universal truths – which is a fact of human being – but to explain this fact, and to give the lesson of this fact. And this lesson is very important, because *if* something like a generic part of humanity exists we must display this part, and we must organize our life by this part.

And so philosophy is not only something abstract, but also something that very concretely can give an orientation to life. We return, finally, again to the beginning: philosophy confirms that true life means that we are not only inside the world as it is, philosophy is what corrupts the corrupted vision that the world as it is is all that there is. Life – *to live* – is not at all always the same. There is an infinite difference between a life which, from beginning to end, is only inside the world as it is – inside some particular culture – and a life which while within a particular culture is also in relationship to something else, not something like a transcendental world, but to something of the infinite creative possibility of human being, a life in relationship to something universal, something true, of something that is beyond the world as it is. True life is precisely a question of creating, of helping to create something that exists for everyone, *today*, *here*, but also in completely other worlds in time and in space....

There are two conceptions of what is a human life, and there is a fight between these two conceptions. The first conception is that human life can be reduced to the question of what is our interest in the world as it is. This is the common conception, the normal conception. But there is another possibility: human life is, certainly, something like that – we have to take care of our interests in the world as it is – but with the possibility of something else. But – I repeat – this possibility is not only a possibility, it's also a fact, because something like that exists – it is a possibility only in the sense that it is a possibility for you to participate, that it exists is a fact. Some men have organized their lives to create something of universal nature, and humanity – in its generic sense – is on *this side, it is on the side of universal creations, on the side of truths.* And so, probably, we too must give our proper contribution to these aspects of the life of humanity. And so we must in this sense, *in this sense...* introduce something of universal nature into our common life, and into our collective life. Philosophy, ultimately, is always a question of accepting that there is something irreducible to our proper interests in the present, and, in fact, something greater.

I think that philosophy is the possibility to rationally explain all of that, and it is why the anthropological nature of philosophy is so complex. If philosophy recognizes the existence of universal truths and if philosophy explains why universal truths exist –

they exist, but philosophy must explain how this is possible, it must explain why such existence is possible – if philosophy is something like that, then *philosophy itself is not reducible to its context*, because the very existence of philosophy is completely dependent on the existence of universal truths, and the resurrection of these truths. Philosophy exists not because society, ordinary life, ordinary language, private interests and so on exist. *No*, philosophy exists because there exist things like the novel of Murasaki Shikibu, things like Greek mathematics, African sculpture and so on. *That is the world of philosophy: the world of philosophy is not reducible to the world as it is, to the concrete and our proper interests in it – the world of philosophy is the world of truths, the world of philosophy is the always of time*!

The world of philosophy is certainly a practical world, but the true world of philosophy is the world of truths, a world the destination of which is beyond our proper interests and beyond the limits of our particular world. And it is not at all the same to be merely a citizen of the world and to be a citizen of humanity. And philosophy *creates something like that*, it creates the possibility of being a citizen of humanity, which is not in contradiction with our proper existence as a citizen of some country, or some culture, but which introduces some exception into particularity.

We are a concrete existence in a determined world, and so we cannot become a pure universality – that is absolutely impossible. But we can introduce into our lives some great moments of exception, where we experiment with the possibility of being a citizen of humanity, on the basis of our proper world and our proper culture. We experience something like that when, in our lives, in our common lives, something happens which cannot be reduced to our ordinary existence – it can be a magnificent book, a painting, a political event, a love... many things, after all.

We have the chance to participate in the creation and resurrection of truths, this chance exits in life itself, and it's a pity to refuse this chance. Thank you.

3. Day Three

3.1 Lecture V

Over these days we will move across three questions, three particular questions: the first was the anthropological nature of philosophy, the second is the dialectical nature of philosophy, and the third will be the paradoxical relationship between philosophy and time. This morning we have come to the second question, the question of the dialectical nature of philosophy.

We have said that the dialectical nature of philosophy is opposed to the idea of analytic philosophy. More generally, this opposition is also the opposition between two conceptions of philosophy: the first is that philosophy, finally, is a knowledge, a knowledge like any other, from mathematics to the human sciences, and the second is that philosophy is in relationship with knowledge. Naturally, philosophy is not outside the question of knowledge. It is possible to say that in classical philosophy, for example, the question of knowledge is the most important question of philosophy – we know something, we can know something, or, finally, we know nothing. Certainly all of that is a great and very old discussion inside of philosophy. We cannot say that philosophy is without relationship to knowledge – that would be completely absurd – but we must ask the question of whether philosophy itself is a knowledge.

As we have seen, when there exists the question of something – the question of what it is – this question, generally speaking, is not inside that something itself. For example, the question 'what is mathematics' is not a mathematical question – it's a philosophical question, in fact. And we have also said that if the question 'what is philosophy' is inside philosophy, then this is a sort of exception... it is an exception. This is because the question 'what is this thing', 'what is this other thing', and so on – this questions of 'what is', in general – is always a philosophical question. It's the question of the very essence of something: what is this something really, what is the sense of this something, of mathematics, but also of nature, of God, and so on. And so, if the question 'what is' is a philosophical question which we can apply to philosophy itself – if the question of 'what is philosophy' is inside philosophy – it is, probably, because philosophy is not exactly a knowledge.

A knowledge is determined by its object – a knowledge is always the knowledge of something, after all. And, naturally, as a knowledge of something it's not reducible to the something itself, because there is necessarily a distance between the knowledge of something and the existence of that something. A knowledge, then, is first the question of its object: what is the object of science, what is the object of physics, what is the object of history, and so on. You understand, then, that it is not possible to say that the question 'what is philosophy' is a question of the knowledge of an object, precisely because philosophy is not an object. And so, if we have a field where the question of itself exists inside of it, this field is not a field of the relationship between knowledge and the thing – its different, its absolutely different.

Concerning this problem we have a very classical tradition, which says that philosophy is not a knowledge, because, precisely, philosophy is a question – the very essence of the existence of philosophy is the existence of some particular questions. This is a very classic affirmation. And, at the beginning of a class of philosophy, the professor will say that philosophy is an infinite question, in fact, that it's not at all some answer but precisely a question. We shall see that this definition is not really precise: philosophy is a question, okay, but there are many fields of human activity where some questions exist and which are not reducible to philosophy. And so, if philosophy is a field of questions it is a field of singular questions and not of questions in general. But, finally, what we must first understand is that philosophy is not an object, and so the fact that 'what is philosophy' is a question inside philosophy means that philosophy cannot be reduced to a knowledge of philosophy, of the history of philosophy. Certainly, philosophy is a question of itself – 'what is philosophy'... – *but it's not reducible to a knowledge of itself.*

The dialectical nature of philosophy means that philosophy is not a positive knowledge, it is not a science – philosophy is something without any object. This conception of philosophy is in a precise opposition to the idea of analytic philosophy, because if we assume the analytical vision of philosophy we propose, in fact, that philosophy is a knowledge, a knowledge with some definite object. For example, it could be the knowledge of language, and so it would have the questions of meaning, of what is a sentence with a meaning, or what is sentence which is non-sense, all of which would constitute a possible field for a specific knowledge, and this knowledge would be philosophy.

For the moment, then, the dialectical vision of philosophy is something purely negative: philosophy is not a knowledge. From this point we can go to the famous affirmation of Socrates: 'the only thing that I know is that I know nothing'... the only thing that I know is that I know nothing.... This is, precisely, a clear affirmation that philosophy is not a knowledge – *'...I know nothing'.* But there is, here, a dialectical ambiguity, because Socrates is also saying that he knows something, *he knows something....* What is that sort of thing? Precisely *nothing.* So, in fact, the sentence of Socrates proposes that at one point something is the same as nothing. Why? Because we can know this 'nothing', and, in fact, it is the unique thing which we can know. We have, here, a sort of equation, *a primitive equation* – and not only in my vision of Socrates, but across the entire great history of philosophy – which is the equivalence of thing and nothing. In philosophy, then, there is a proposition of the possibility of an absolutely paradoxical equivalence, the equivalence of thing and nothing.

For philosophy there is the possibility to examine this sort of equivalence. But what sort of question is this? This question is the question of negativity, it is the question of negation, of the function of nothingness, and so on. What Socrates proposed – when he made the equation between thing and nothing, when he said that *he could know nothing* – is, maybe, that if philosophy is not a knowledge, it's precisely because the object of philosophy is not a thing – it is not a country, it is not nature, it is not some physical object, and so on. The great question of philosophy is the question of nothingness, the question of the existence of negativity. And this is why, form the very beginning, there is a close relationship between the dialectical nature of philosophy and the question of negativity. Philosophy is the question of negativity in all of its aspects – the question of the relation between thing and nothing, the question of the existence of nothingness, of the paradoxical existence of nothingness.

There is something like a hidden affirmation in philosophy – across the entire history of philosophy – which comes out of the question of negativity: is it possible to know something which does not exist... is it possible to think something which does not exist.... And so, why is philosophy not a knowledge? Because the answer to this question is certainly *not that there is a knowledge of something that does not exist* – if something exists, then there is a specific knowledge of that sort of thing, whatever it may be – some natural object, some psychological state, and so on. But if something does not exist, then the relationship to this non-existence cannot be a knowledge, because knowledge is a knowledge of an object, and something which does not exist is not an object.

And so the existence of philosophy is always also the question of the possibility of something that does not exist, something that does not exist as an object, as an object of the world. And so we can say that philosophy is entirely based on a difference – a very obscure and complex difference – between to be and to exist. This question of the distance between to be and to exist is also, naturally, the question of the distance between thing and nothing, the distance between being and nothingness, and so on. I say all of this in order to give you an idea of the dialectical nature of philosophy: the dialectical nature of philosophy is to not be reducible to the question of the knowledge of an object, but to introduce the possibility of the being of something which does not exist, which is not in the form of an object and which can be affirmed in its presence, in its being, outside the form of knowledge of an object.

We can name positivism – which is a sort of anti-philosophical philosophy – the affirmation that there exists only knowledge, and that the idea of a distance between to be and to exist, or the thesis that there is something which is equivalent to nothing, are absurd. Positivism affirms that the only things which exist are those which are in the form of objectivity, and that our relationship to objectivity is knowledge. Finally, it is the affirmation that the true form of knowledge is science. This is the definition, the clear definition, of positivism. The positivist proposes that all that exists is objectively existent... that *this is the only form of being*, and that the only form of positive relationship to objectivity is knowledge, and, finally, science. So the positivist conclusion is: either philosophy is a science or philosophy does not exist, and philosophy is imaginary, illusion and so on, a pure faith, a pure faith without any objective value. In fact, positivism is – in my conviction – the only consistent form of the analytic point of view – if you are in the analytic point of view you must, finally, be a positivist. If you are a positivist, you must say that in the form of knowledge we have our only rational relationship to what exits, and you must affirm – because its the case in the contemporary world – that the real and efficient form of knowledge is science. And so, if we were positivists we would have to say that the ideal of philosophy is science – philosophy must become a science. And, if this is not the case – if philosophy does not reach the ideal of science – then philosophy must be criticized, and, finally, it must be suppressed. True positivism affirms the necessity to restitute all forms of knowledge to the field of science, and philosophy – dialectical philosophy – and precisely metaphysics, is something like a dream, something like a dream, an imaginary dream.

Naturally, the problem with that sort of assertion is of philosophical nature: positivism is, finally, itself not a science. And why is it not a science? It is not a science because there does not exist a science of sciences, there does not exists a science which says what is science. And so, when the positivist says 'all that really exists is science, and we must transform philosophy into the form of science,' he says it not from a position inside of a science, but from a position that is, finally, inside philosophy. And so, we can reply to the positivist with a proper question: from what position can you say that that sort of process is a science and that sort of process is not a science? If all knowledge is science, then knowledge of what is a science must also be a science. And so, the positivist, in fact, affirms the existence of a science of sciences. But a science of sciences does not really exist, or, if something like that exists then it is philosophy. And why? Because to affirm something as the science of sciences we would have to discern what is the real being of science and not only the existence of science.

We know that there exists mathematics, biology, physics, and so on, history, scientific history maybe, but when we say that all that is of scientific nature we are saying something concerning all sciences and so something which is not inside any particular science – a science does not propose why it is a science. When we say that an existing science is a science we say it not from the strict point of view of their existence but from the point of view of their being – we say: *they are* sciences. What exists is not the science, but many sciences, many different sciences. And so when we say that there is something which is common across all sciences, what authorizes us to say that all of this is of scientific nature is not a question of existence, but precisely a question of being. You understand? And so the distance between to be and to exist is in fact assumed by the positivist. And if the question of the distance between to be and to exist is of dialectical nature, then it's impossible to reduce all that the positivist proposes, all that he affirms – including the position from which he speaks – to the analytic point of view. Therefore, there is something dialectical in positivism itself.

All that is a proof of what? All that is a proof that, ultimately, positivists assume a part of philosophy. Strict positivism assumes – *and it must assume* –a part of philosophy, or, if you want, the analytical vision must assume a part of the dialectical vision. And when is there such a necessity? Precisely when the analytical point of view affirms the analytical point of view, because the dialectical position is a necessity precisely when you are in the analytical point of view. If you are a positivist, then when you make your affirmation – when you say that there is nothing other than what exists objectively, than what can be known – you also affirm something else... you also say something else. In fact, when you say that the analytical point of view is true and the dialectical point of view is false, you are saying something which is in the dialectical point of view, *by necessity, by necessity*! Why? Because you assume the distinction between to be and to exist, you assume it because you assume a position from which you can affirm what is the being of science, the being of science as it is common across all sciences.

And so, the opposition between the dialectical point of view and the analytical point of view is dialectical. When the analytical philosopher criticizes the dialectical philosopher he is inside the dialectical point of view, he cannot be inside a purely analytical point of view. In the purely analytical point of view you cannot be in the form of negativity, and so, if you say something negative you are in contradiction with yourself. If you say 'the dialectical point of view is not true', the 'not true', naturally, assumes the distinction between what exists and what *is,* because the dialectical point of view exists. And so, if you say that it's false, you are saying something concerning not its existence but its being, naturally, because we cannot say that the dialectical point of view does not exists, its exists. When the positivist says that the dialectical position exists but is false, he is saying something that is not reducible to the question of existence or non-existence – to be and to exist are not on the same level. This is a proof, its a proof, it's a dialectical proof, but it's a proof. It's a proof that positivism exists but that it assumes – by necessity – a small part of dialecticity as a point of view, not as a pure existence, naturally. So, when the analytical point of view criticizes the dialectical point of view it necessarily assumes something of the dialectical point of view itself.

This is, again, why the question of negativity is always at the very beginning of philosophy itself.

We have two fundamental examples of this beginning in negativity: Socrates and Plato, and Descartes. Socrates – as we have said – announced 'the only thing that I know is that I know nothing'. This affirmation places the question of negativity into the first sentence of philosophy... because he proposed an equivalence, a possible equivalence, of thing and nothing – 'the only thing that I know is that I know nothing'. And so, finally, the first proposition of Socrates – at the very beginning of philosophy, *as the very beginning of philosophy* – is that there is a possible equivalence of thing and nothing. And to say that there is a possible equivalence of thing and nothing, is to say that something can be and not exist. We have, here, a very profound and original point – you understand. *This question of the distance between to be and to exist is really the philosophical question.*

There are, naturally, many ways to say that there exists this distance. But to say that there is this distance – between to be and to exist – finally, is purely abstract, and says nothing of the distance itself. And so, when we affirm this distance, we affirm it, in fact, as a question, as a question.... And, finally, this is why – throughout its history – philosophy is in a relationship to ontology.

If we name ontology.... Ontology is a word, which like many, many others, was created by Aristotle – Aristotle the man of classifications, the great creator of the discourse of the university, who invented many words of traditional, classical *and* modern philosophy. So, what is ontology? Ontology – as you know – is the science of being as such, the science of being *qua* being. It is the proposition of a complete science of the verb 'to be', the complete science of the signification of this verb. There is always a part of ontology in any philosophy, and this part is precisely the possibility of giving signification to the distance between to be and to exist. Ontology affirms that to be is not reducible to what we know to exist as an object in the world. And so, the question of the distance between to be and to exist is of ontological nature – in the sense of Aristotle – and it is absolutely at the very core of the dialectical vision. And this distance, this irreducibility, is always at the beginning of a philosophy – we find it at the beginning of Plato, as the beginning of Descartes, at the beginning of Kant and Heidegger also, at the beginning of Deleuze, and me, it is the same in each case.

At the beginning we cannot say anything concerning being as such, because it's not a knowledge. And, in fact, when something is not a knowledge you cannot continue by transmission. In some sense, this point is difficult and obscure. If something is a knowledge then you can have a teacher, a professor, who transmits this knowledge which you don't then have, and this knowledge – knowledge itself doesn't really begin – then continues by successive transmissions. So what is transmission? Transmission is always a transmission of the state of a knowledge, the contemporary state of a knowledge. Maybe you – for didactic reasons – begin at a sort of beginning, but, finally, the transmission is the transmission of a knowledge as such, and knowledge itself does not begin, it continues. And so a transmission of knowledge is, in fact, always in the form of repetition or continuation – it is a continuity of knowledge because knowledge is cumulative. There is, for example, Greek mathematics and, after that, you *continue* that knowledge.

But why is it that we can continue a knowledge? It is because a knowledge has a precise object, and so you have a field, you have an objectivity, and in relationship to this objectivity you have successive progressions in that knowledge. And so the ideology, the positivist ideology of progress, of continuity and so on, is absolutely in relationship to the definition of knowledge itself. And so, knowledge continues, history continues, physics continues, and so on. And we can speak of progress, of a continuing progress of some knowledge, and we can speak of the transmission of the contemporary state of problems and solutions in an objective field of knowledge.

Philosophy, on the other hand – if philosophy is not a knowledge

– cannot properly continue.... *Philosophy always begins.* Philosophy always begins, and philosophy always begins by assuming its past, it assumes its past as a sort of succession of beginnings – Plato begins, Aristotle begins, Descartes begins, Kant and others begin. Philosophy is always a beginning of philosophy, with a past, but a past composed of beginnings. And so the question of the beginning is a very important question in philosophy.

A philosophy begins, but how can we begin a philosophy? What is a beginning of a philosophy? What is the beginning of Socrates, the beginning of Plato, *if they don't continue something*? What is the beginning if a philosopher does not begin by a continuation, if he does not say 'okay we know this, we know that, and so on, and we will continue this knowledge, and we will come to know something else'? This is never the case. In fact, if you read a book of philosophy it never says 'all the philosophers before me knew something, proved something, and so we have this knowledge, and I will continue this knowledge'. No, never...never. Every philosopher has said: 'I begin, I begin... there is a great history, but I cannot continue all of that, and so I must begin again'. In this sense, philosophy is absolutely different from positive knowledge – there is no continuity, properly speaking. Instead, what we find in the history of philosophy – in its relation to its own past – is a sequence of new interpretations of this past. And we can, absolutely, begin with a new interpretation of Plato, a new interpretation of Aristotle, and so on. But our beginning is not Plato's, it cannot be Aristotle's. Our beginning – the beginning of every new philosophy – is not a continuation of the past, but a new interpretation of this past.

But we must ask: how is some interpretation new? It is new if it begins something, if it begins something new. But what exactly is a beginning? We know what a beginning is in a knowledge, because we can know the objectivity of that knowledge. But, in philosophy – if philosophy is, finally, the creation of a new subjective desire and so on – what is a beginning? And how can we begin something of dialectical nature, something which is in relationship to negativity? We must begin by negativity – that is the only possible conclusion. Why? Precisely because *we cannot begin by an object,* by a positive object – we cannot begin with an object because we are not in a field of knowledge. And so, we must begin with negativity.

We must begin exactly as Socrates said: we must begin by nothing, we must begin *in nothing.* And, as we know, practically all of the great philosophers began by nothingness, *in* nothingness. *The only thing that I know is that I know nothing ...I know nothing!* There is, after all, a positive affirmation in Socrates, in this negative beginning: I cannot know a thing, *but I know nothing.* But what is the sense of 'I know nothing'? It's really obscure – 'I know nothing'.... Can you represent the signification of something like that, of the attempt to know nothing?

At the beginning of a philosophy is not a knowledge. And when Socrates says 'I know nothing' its a joke, naturally, its a verbal joke – 'the only thing I know is that I know nothing', its a joke, a verbal joke. The reality is that it's impossible to know nothing. The relationship to nothingness is not a knowledge, but an experience, a subjective experience. And the form of this primitive experience is very fundamental in the differences between philosophies. For example, you know that the experience of nothingness in Descartes is the duped, the absolute duped – 'I know nothing, really, I know nothing'. But 'I know nothing' cannot be a knowledge, and so the duped is a pure subjectivity – to 'know nothing' is an experience. And to be really duped is not easy, it is very difficult, in fact. It is not the imaginary experience of 'ok, I can picture it: I am in my chair, I am duped, I know nothing'. No, it is a traumatic experience, it's a subjective experience, which must be a *real experience*: I myself must have the concrete experience of being totally duped – and it is a traumatic experience – it is, finally, something like the destruction of a world, of my world, a subjective destruction of the world.

As a philosopher I must go to this experience – this subjective experience where all is nonsense, where I know nothing – and it's not easy, its not something that I can just write in a dissertation – 'I know nothing...'. If it's something like that, then it's a joke, then it's nothing at all. And so, the duped – the Cartesian duped, the duped of the great rationalism of Descartes – is existential in nature, it is not at all a rational moment. And so there is something dramatic, something purely subjective, something negative – a negative experience – and, finally, something existential, at the beginning of what may come to be a reconstruction of the possibility o knowledge. And, in fact, the subject – the primitive philosophical subject – is negativity. The subjective dimension of philosophy is precisely the negative dimension – it is not reducible to an object, to a positive object, it is the subjective experience of the *power* of negativity. You must understand that you can be in the situation of the totally duped only if it is an experience, a personal experience. In Kierkegaard and Heidegger it is precisely that sort of experience which is the experience of anxiety. It is not at all a positive experience, a clear movement of the discovery of something, no, it's the power of negativity, and when we are really in the position of the totally duped we don't *know* if its possible to go beyond. Maybe we stay in the duped, maybe we stay in anxiety, maybe we stay in that sort of radical experience of negativity – it is a possibility... there is a risk.

And so the beginning of philosophy is something subjective, something existential, something like a radical experience, and it is why philosophy cannot continue at an individual level. Naturally, you can prepare, you can read books – you must, you must read the books of some great philosophers, and so on – but that cannot be the beginning of philosophy, precisely because all of that is history – the history of philosophy, maybe – and so it is a positive knowledge. To know the history of philosophy cannot on its own be the beginning of philosophy, and so we must affirm that philosophy cannot begin by books alone.

This experience – and, certainly, it can be many different experiences after all – is something which happens, it is not something that we decide – decide clearly by some rational decision – it is something which happens. And you can see that the duped in Descartes is a sort of story, a subjective story: for a long time there is no duped in Descartes, and Descartes is only continuing scholastic philosophy, and then, one day, one night, something happens. There is something like conversion, something like a subjective transformation, at the beginning of philosophy. And this transformation is always in the form of some negative experience – it cannot be the experience of some positive object, or the experience of some situation, it is, across all instances, a pure experience of some negativity, of the possibility of nothingness.

As you all know other forms of Socrates' sentence – 'the only thing that I know is that I know nothing' – are found in the famous quotations of many philosophies. Leibniz, for example, says: 'why is there something and not nothing?' And why, in fact, is there something rather than nothing? Why does something exist? Why does anything exist? Why we are not in nothingness? Is there any reason for this? Technically, in Leibniz this is the question of the principle of sufficient reason... the principle of sufficient reason: the principle which explains that if something exists there is a reason for its existence, that there is a reason which explains why this thing exists. But, finally, the great question concerning the principle of sufficient reason is: why is there a reason for the existence of something? Or: why is there something and not nothing... why we are not?

This question is not purely the question of the possibility of nothingness, but the question of the possibility of the nothingness of existence *from the point of view of being*: if we say that existence is absurd, we necessarily say this from the point of view of being, from inside the distance between to be and to exist. This is another form of the negative beginning of philosophy – there is always a negativity at the beginning, it is a condition of philosophy, and so philosophy must always begin. Without such a moment – where there is the possibility of the complete non-sense of existence, the complete nothingness of signification, the complete nothingness of existence itself – philosophy cannot begin. And so – if for the moment we name the experience of this nothingness anxiety – we could define a philosophy as something like a form of subjective victory over anxiety.

In Husserl we find a very similar experience: *epoché* – *epoché* is the Greek word for the suspension, the interruption of any relation to objectivity. At this moment I decide that objectivity is illusion, that it is not here, that it does not exist, and so I reduce all existence to my pure perception of it – there is not objectivity before me. Such an experience, naturally, is also a purely negative experience, and very much like the one of Descartes, it is an experience of pure subjectivity. The pure experience of subjectivity is always the pure experience of nothingness, because it's subjectivity without objectivity, so it's a negation of the entire field of objectivity. You understand that by necessity the beginning of philosophy – if philosophy is not a knowledge, like science – is in negativity, because philosophy cannot be the development of a knowledge of objectivity. If knowledge continues it is because it is guaranteed by objectivity, and so without the guarantee of objectivity there is no knowledge, there is pure subjectivity, and pure subjectivity is the experience of something *without* objective existence.

So you understand that, finally, it's something like the experience of pure being, pure being as apart from existence. And this is exactly the conclusion of Descartes, it is the victory of Descartes against the duped: the victory of Descartes is the affirmation that something *is, that something really is*. And what is? Subjectivity itself, the duped itself.

When Descartes, by the affirmation of the existence of the subject – the subject who is in the duped, and who exists if the duped exists – goes beyond the duped he affirms the existence of something within negativity, he affirms from within negativity that something really is. And what? The experience itself. And so, the existence of the experience of negativity is the victory against pure negativity. It is the same in Socrates, logically... the only thing that I know is that I know nothing. Finally, you go from nothing to thing. This is the fundamental gesture of philosophy: the possibility – at the moment of the pure experience of negativity – to go from nothingness to existence, or, if you want, to go from being to existence, from the pure being of something which does not exist to something which exists, from the duped to the existence of the subject of the duped, and so on.

There are many forms of this movement, because there are many beginnings, many philosophers, finally. And so, while there are many forms of that process, there is a general abstract form, which is the movement where something can transit from nothingness to the affirmation of some existence, from pure being to existence, or from experience – the dramatic existence of nothingness – to the clear affirmation of the existence, the certainty of the existence of something. *And that is*, if you want, *the first victory of philosophy.* If there is no such victory, then you are in a form of anti-philosophical philosophy, then you are in another form of anti-philosophical philosophy, which is nihilism... nihilism.

What is nihilism? Nihilism is, finally, the proposition that we cannot go beyond the experience of negativity. In Cartesian language it is the duped, the duped without God, the duped without the existence of supreme subjectivity. We now have two enemies of philosophy, two different enemies, two contrary enemies of philosophy. The first enemy of philosophy is positivism, all forms of positivism – 'the only serious thing is knowledge, and finally, philosophy is a collection of jokes, and non-sense'. Sometimes, you will find something like that in Wittgenstein: all propositions of metaphysics are non-sense, all such suppositions are, ultimately, imaginary, philosophy is a fantasy, and, finally, philosophy is something like myth, like some beautiful stories, and so on, but it's not serious ... it's not serious. The second enemy of philosophy is nihilism, a nihilism which is, finally, more profound than skepticism. Nihilism is precisely the conviction that there is something which is not knowledge, and it is the proposition that it is knowledge which is not serious, which is imaginary, and so on. And so, it is the complete reverse of positivism. For a true nihilist what is important is, precisely, the subjective experience. And this moment of the subjective experience of negativity, of nothingness, is the common point between nihilism and philosophy. If you want, we can say that what is common to nihilism and philosophy is that both are a critique of positivism, and for both the first moment is this critique, which is the radical subjective experience of nothingness.

But philosophy cannot be reduced to nihilism, because nihilism is also the conviction that the experience of negativity cannot be interrupted. For nihilism we *stay in the experience of negativity,* we *stay in anxiety, anxiety is our world, it is our destiny*, and there is no future, there is no knowledge. If you want, the nihilist says: 'I must only exist, I must only exist in nothingness itself, so I must drink, enjoy, enjoy the nothingness'. Nihilism is a very strong position, today, but also before. We must understand, and we must understand very clearly, that philosophy's opposition to nihilism is not the same as its opposition to positivism. In fact, the two are very much contradictory oppositions. I think that positivism is the position on the right of philosophy and nihilism is the position of the ultra left. Nihilism is a radical ultra leftist position: it mistakes the radial experience, and states that we cannot go beyond it, that we cannot affirm anything, that there is only negativity... only negativity.

Philosophy, properly, is neither positivism nor nihilism. Philosophy tries to open the possibility of a thinking that is not reducible to knowledge or positivism, but not reducible to the primitive experience of negativity either, even if this experience is a necessity for philosophy itself. And so, the fundamental position of philosophy is that we have the possibility go outside the experience of negativity, to go beyond it, to go, finally, from being to existence. Nihilism, naturally, responds by saying: 'nothing exists, and my being is to affirm the fundamental in-existence of everything – all that exists is existence itself, the experience of existence'.

And so the beginning of philosophy is nihilism – in some sense – but we must go across nihilism. Without some experience of nihilism, there is, I think, no philosophy at all – we must know what is anxiety, we must know what is the experience of nothingness, we must be open to the possibility of nothingness, because if we do not open the possibility of nothingness there is pure objectivity and knowledge, and nothing else, no philosophy, in fact, no serious philosophy. Philosophy is serious *because* of the experience of nothingness at the beginning, without it, it is only academic, reducible to knowledge – without nihilism it is scholasticism. But philosophy is also the idea that we can go beyond nihilism. And it can go beyond by the affirmation that truths exist, that there is something like truths, that there is a positive affirmation of existence. And so, we must fully understand the distance between being and existence – it is the very place of philosophy, what must be divided by philosophy, and, also, what must be traversed by philosophy.

For nihilism there is no understanding of all that, there is only the experience, the living experience, of nothingness, and it is the last word of nihilism. But for philosophy this is not the last word – certainly, we must have that sort of experience, we must, *but we must, and we can*, also go beyond it. In fact, it is only by going beyond nihilism that we can find a true understanding of that distance, the negative distance between to be and to exist, and, finally, have a thought of the negativity and not only an experience of it. The movement of philosophy is, therefore, also this movement from experience to thinking. We can say that positivism is thinking without the experience of negativity, and nihilism the experience of negativity without thinking. Within these two possibilities, we have, in some sense, the space of our determination, our vital determination.

Finally, we can say that for humanity there exist three positions, and everyone must choose. There is the positivist position: one must be and exist in the world as it is, with knowledge, technology and interests, and one must be positive... be positive – one must be a positivist. The second position is nihilism: one must accept that all that there is is the experience, the experience of nothingness, of anxiety, the experience of pure life, as, in fact, pure nothingness, and one must enjoy, that is all that one can do – in the end, finally, nihilism is life under the power of death. The third position I name the philosophical one. And we must understand that philosophy, in this sense of a position in life, is something much more important than pure philosophical discourse. And, in fact, the positivist position too is much more important than pure positivism: it is, in fact, the position of ordinary contemporary life, which is something like resignation, like the acceptance of the closure of knowledge, the acceptance of something like the closure of the world. The second position – which is extremist, in some sense – is a refusal of the world as it is, and a resignation to negativity, to nothingness, because there is no beyond. And as a position of life nihilism too is more important, because it is the complete refusal of the world as it is, of the positive experience of the world as it is: it is a radical critique of the world as it is, in some sense, but without the possibility of something else, without the possibility of another world, and so, it is a refusal of the idea that within the world as it is there exists a possibility of another world. And philosophy – the philosophical life – is to assume the *necessity* of nihilistic experience but to simultaneously affirm that we must, and so, that we can, go beyond this sort of experience. The philosophical position, therefore, is that we can go beyond the experience of pure negativity to a positive affirmation which is *outside*, or which is other to, positivism.

The beginning of philosophy, then, is negativity, but the great question of philosophy is affirmation – the beginning is a rupture with the positivist position, but the great question is the rupture with nihilism. This is the double fight of philosophy, the double fight of philosophy against the positivist resignation but also against nihilism as the impossibility of affirmation.

You will find this double fight in every philosophy. And, in fact, it is another way in which to read philosophers: we can ask where is the fight against positivism and where is the fight against nihilism in any particular philosophy. We could even say that you can find the singularity of a philosophy by the articulation of these two great fights. For example, some philosophies propose that the critique of positivism is much important than the critique of nihilism, others say the reverse, and so on and so on – there are many possibilities. Maybe we could say that a system of philosophy is like a musical symphony: in a musical symphony there are two essential moments, there is the rupture with silence and there is return to the silence, there is a break at both ends. Music, in all its forms, is also a double fight: the fight of the organization of the music itself, the structure of the music itself, against the silence, which is at the beginning – you begin all music in silence, naturally, since it is impossible to begin music by another manner – but its also, always, the preparation of the return of the silence, which is the end. The question in music, in fact, is largely that of the beginning and of the end, with some movement between the two, a movement which is a movement from silence to silence. And so, in music too we can find a double fight: the fight against the idea of the pure silence of the world, if you want, the nothingness of all noise, and on the other side we have the organization of an affirmation of the other form of silence, the silence that is inside of music itself. And this is why it is difficult to finish a composition – and this is true of every form of music: there is music which continues indefinitely, there is music which makes a brutal end, and there is music which prepares the end, repeatedly, or even music which is just a long preparation of the end. In Beethoven, for example, there is the end, and then the end, and then the end, and another end... and, finally, the true end, at the end, after all. But also in jazz, for example, the question of the structure of the end is precisely the norm of the history of jazz. At the beginning of jazz – with the New Orleans style, Armstrong, and so on – there is something very coded: you have a definition of the theme, variation and then the end. But in Coltrane, on the other hand, the end becomes absolutely erratic, there is no end at all, in fact. But why do I mention all of this? Because it is exactly the same in philosophy: there is a double fight – in music, and in philosophy – and there are different forms of organizing the double fight, there is the fight against silence at the beginning and the fight against silence at the end, and they are not the same thing at all, they are contradictory fights.

So my proposition is for you to read philosophy in the manner that you listen to music, and so to have a sensibility not only for the rational and conceptual organization of philosophy – which is very important, naturally – but also for something which is like the tonality of a philosophy, which is always in relationship to the tonality of nihilism and the tonality of positivism.

In some cases this suggestion is absolutely clear: you know perfectly well that you immediately find the relationship to nihilism in Kierkegaard's theory of anxiety, or in the theory of eternal return in Nietzsche. So there are philosophies which have the tonality of nihilism immediately and clearly present, and, on the other side, there are philosophies where the tonality of positivism is clearly and immediately present – with positive knowledge, and so on – and you find that in Aristotle and Searle, for example. The true reading of a philosopher is precisely to find the tonality which is not the obvious tonality: it is to find the nihilism in Descartes, for example, or to find not nihilism in Kierkegaard – which is not very difficult – but the positivism of Kierkegaard, to find the affirmations of Kierkegaard – and that is difficult to find.

The understanding of a great philosopher is always the understanding of the two tonalities, and, certainly, there is always, in every *philosophy*, a tonality which is more important than the other. You know that in the history of philosophy, in philosophers like Hume or Kierkegaard, Nietzsche or Heidegger, the nihilist tonality is absolutely present, you can find that without any difficulty. And so the true reading is to find in them the other tonality! In Aristotle, Descartes or Spinoza, on the other hand, naturally, the rationalist and positivist tonality is clearly present, and so, to find the nihilist moment is the true reading. Finally, we must affirm that it is important to read philosophers in the dialectical manner, that is, to find contradictory tonalities in the development of a philosophy. And why? Because there is a double fight: philosophy is against positivism and against nihilism, and against positivism it is with nihilism, and against nihilism it is, in some sense, with positivism. But the movement, the fundamental movement, is the movement to go beyond nihilism because the beginning is always in nihilism itself, the beginning is always some experience of negativity.

You can take, for example, the case of Kant, which is a rational critique of all the pretensions of classical metaphysics and so on, and which is the beginning of the modern critique – Kant is, after all, the beginning of the end of classical metaphysics. But the beginning of Kant is absolutely negative: all that philosophy has affirmed concerning God and nature is illusion, all of it is imaginary, it's false, and we cannot know real being, we cannot know what they really are, what they are in themselves. This is the first fundamental affirmation of Kant! So the first experience of Kant is not at all a clear and rational experience, no! The first experience is of a negative nature: our dream to really know the distance between to be and to exist, between things-in-themselves and as they appear to us, our dream to really be in that sort of reality is, finally, absolutely impossible. And so, the beginning of Kant is also a traumatic experience of theoretical anxiety: Kant's problem at the beginning is, finally, that if he cannot know being as such, then what is the status of our knowledge? After that Kant reconstructs the possibility of a sort of knowledge – which is the affirmative part of his construction, the positivist part, finally – but the beginning itself is purely of negative nature! And so – we can stop here for the moment – we can define philosophy as a primitive movement from pure

negativity to a first affirmation, to a first affirmation just after
the nihilist temptation... – philosophy is the movement from the
nihilist temptation to a first affirmation. In Descartes, for
example, this first affirmation is the affirmation of the real
existence of the subject itself, and after that Descartes
reconstructs all of the world, all knowledge, all positivity. The
simple representation of philosophy is something like this:

$$\mathbf{0} \to 1$$

This is a schema, the schema of philosophy. The problem, the
great problem, is: what exactly is 0, and what exactly is 1? 0 is
the emblem of the nihilist experience, the nihilist experience of
nothingness and negativity, and it's the true beginning, and 1 is
the emblem of the first affirmation. But we can also – by an
ontological projection – say that the movement in philosophy is
this:

$$\varnothing \to \omega$$

Maybe, philosophy is this movement: the movement from the
anti-set to omega, to the infinite, the first infinite. We stop here.

3.2 Lecture VI

The dialectical nature of philosophy defines philosophy as not merely pure theory but as a movement, a real movement, a movement that creates, that establishes, new possibilities in thinking. The scheme proposed in the last lesson ($\varnothing \to \omega$) is the inscription of this movement.

If philosophy was only on the side of zero, on the side of the void, it would, in fact, be nihilism. The nihilistic position – we have seen – is precisely the proposition that there is only experience, the pure experience of the void of existence, and that there is no name, and that any affirmative or constructive knowledge is impossible. On the other hand, if philosophy was only on the side of the one or omega – as a symbol for the infinite – then, finally, philosophy would be either positivism or positivist theology, that is, it would be on the side of the metaphysics of God. But philosophy is neither of these, it is a movement, it is the movement from the nihilist position to the affirmative position – it is not reducible to either of the two positions. And this is why in the Hegelian tradition – but it was also the position of Heraclitus at the very beginning – philosophy is movement, *it's a movement.* And this is also why we have a beginning and a goal: a beginning in the experience of negativity and the goal of the transformation of subjectivity – the corruption of young people, after all....

Naturally this movement has different stages, different steps. It is not a pure gesture, nor an immediate passage from negativity to affirmation, from the void to the infinite. And so, we have – in the dialectical conception of philosophy – the question of the different moments of the construction of a new affirmation. Between the beginning and the goal we have a sequence of different steps, different moments of this movement. And when we speak of these different steps, we are speaking about something like a decomposition of the movement:

$$\emptyset \rightarrow | \rightarrow | \rightarrow | \rightarrow | \rightarrow | \rightarrow \ldots \ldots \ldots \omega$$

It is these moments – constitutive of the movement from the void to the infinite – which make philosophy systematic. And why is it that philosophy exists only in systematic form? Precisely because we cannot reduce the movement of philosophy to a pure intuition, a pure instance, a pure revelation – *philosophy is not mysticism!*

We can name mysticism the idea that the movement from inside nihilism to infinite affirmation is a single experience. Mysticism is the idea that it is the same experience, the same movement, which goes immediately across nihilism to the infinite itself. There is a description of this sort of experience in the great mystics, in Saint Simon Lacroix, for example, but also in some parts of oriental wisdom. We cannot say that this mystical movement does not exist – it exists. And, in fact, in some sense mysticism is near philosophy: they have a common origin, and a common end. The difference is that in mysticism this movement is a pure experience, something outside of language, and, in fact, outside of transmission, outside of rational transmission. Ultimately, mysticism is the idea of a pure and immediate experience of the infinite from inside nothingness.

As you know, the great mystic poems describe precisely such experiences: they describe the nothingness of pure existence, and, in that sort of destruction of themselves, a pure access to the glory of the infinite. Generally this infinite accessed by the mystic takes the name 'God' – omega as God. We can represent the movement of mysticism like this:

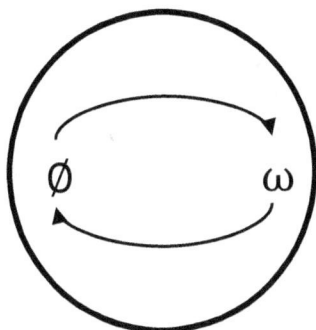

In mysticism we are nothing from the point of the infinite, *but* we can have a pure access to the infinite through the complete realization of our nothingness. If we accept our concrete finitude and nothingness, if we accept to be nothing in regard to the infinite, we open an immediate access to the infinite itself, and we come into a relationship with this infinite. In fact it is a close and intimate relationship, a personal relationship with the infinite. This sort of experience is often described as a love experience. It's not at all a linguistic or rational experience, but a pure experience, where we – by an absolute acceptance of our nothingness – open an access to the infinite. In return we experience the love of God for us – *that* is the prize, finally. And, certainly, it is a very beautiful and magnificent experience. I don't know the experience as such... but I can read about it....

The expression of that sort of experience is of poetical nature, always. The great poems of the great mystics are magnificent pieces of literature, certainly. And we can perfectly understand why: if the experience is an experience of love and not at all an experience which is determined by a rational movement, then the natural inscription of such an experience cannot be a treatise, a system, or a construction, and so on, but the poem, a pure writing, a creation. If we are in the world of mysticism we are in a world organized by the relationship between love and art. We will return to all the problems that follow from such a position.

There is absolutely no relationship to science and politics in mysticism. The relationship between the finite and infinite is completely enclosed by love and art. Love, in fact, is the experience itself. It is really is an experience of love: the infinite's love for the finite, God's love of creation, and so on. But it is a love that can be experienced only if creation accepts that it is only creation. In mysticism love is an interpretation of the experience of nothingness before God, an experience which is immediately also an intense experience of God's love of creation. And it is, certainly, very beautiful, but we understand that it's also a closure – and *this* is the difference with philosophy. It is not a critique to say that.

It's a representation, a personal representation of the experience of a sort of negativity that is enclosed, finally, in the potency of the infinite, for example, in God – if God is the name of the infinite. Naturally, there are different names for the infinite – the name of that sort of experience isn't by necessity God. And it's an experience we find in many cultures, in very different cultures, and in very different religious contexts.

Mysticism

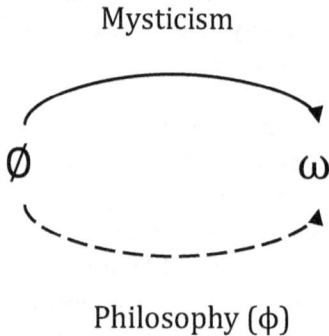

Philosophy (ɸ)

And, as you know, it is another possibility by which to go beyond nihilism, another possibility than philosophy.

We know that if the first point (ᴐ) is isolated we have nihilism. And if the second point (ω) is isolated we have two possibilities: positivism and theology, but theology in rational form, *as a knowledge*, precisely. A rational theology organizes the possibility of a rational representation of God and so on. And so we have two possibilities for this movement (ᴐ→ω): mysticism and philosophy (φ).

Mysticism, therefore, affirms the religious question of going beyond nihilism, but not in the form of a rational and transmissible construction. Rather, it is a matter of finding an access, an opening, from inside the pure experience itself. And so, in some sense, it is a nihilism which transforms itself into something absolute – it reaches the absolute through the pure experience of nothingness. It is a possibility, but it is, finally, an absolutely closed possibility because the mystic is alone, absolutely alone. And this is the problem, *the limit*, of mysticism: a mystic is in a form of radical solitude, radical solitude with God – and God is a strange companion! In fact, this is precisely what mystics themselves say: 'God is a strange companion'. And, very often, mystics will say that they cannot fully describe this experience – there exist some poems, naturally, but they are just approximations and not the true articulation of the experience. The true experience is... they cannot describe the pure experience, there can be no full transmission, and this is why mysticism is a pure solitude. The true experience as such is a revelation, and so it cannot be described by any rational or transmissible means. And so the mystic always faces a choice, a radical choice: to be with God and not with the world, and, finally, not with other people, or to be with the world, to be with others but without God. The mystic is alone, absolutely alone... with God. And the effect of mysticism, finally, is something like a pure effect of attraction. There is a description of this experience in Bergson, in *Les Deux Source de la Morale et de la Religion*.

Les Deux Source de la Morale et de la Religion is a fundamental work of Bergson, and there we find a description of the position of mysticism: Bergson explains that the position of mysticism is not a position which can be transmitted or described, but that there is a particular kind of action, a kind of affect, on other people by the mystic, and that it is a pure attraction, by pure example. It is very difficult to understand, but the idea is that we an have access to the experience by a sort of attraction, something like the effect of the sun on the movement of the sea, or of the moon on the movement of the sea. It is something like elevation, finally, an elevation in the direction – the obscure direction – of the mystic. But, finally, it is purely individual, it is a purely individual destiny, it is a purely singular encounter of one person with God. It is, then, something like an event, but a purely personal event, and it is only by chance – maybe by grace – that one can have that sort of experience. It is, finally, very difficult to say something concerning mysticism because there is really a part of all that which is completely obscure in the closure of pure subjectivity... in the closure of pure subjectivity.... But it is, in some sense, the same movement as philosophy. And so, mysticism is something like philosophy *immediately*, philosophy without patience, without work, without labor – it is like philosophy, but reduced to a pure moment.

Finally, because mysticism is absolutely not reducible to nihilism – it is a very specific experience of nothingness which is immediately, and in the same intimate movement, transformed into a relationship with the infinite – and yet it is not philosophy either – it is not a step-by-step rational construction of this movement, in fact, we can say that mysticism is exactly the opposite of a system – we have four distinct possibilities: positivism, nihilism, mysticism and philosophy.

If we now return to philosophy, we must understand that philosophy is not mysticism. But the relationship between philosophy and mysticism is not at all the same as the relationship between philosophy and nihilism or positivism. Philosophy is not against mysticism – the criticism of mysticism, the destruction of mysticism, is not a task of philosophy – because they are, in some sense, the same movement. If mysticism exists this is not a problem for philosophy. In fact, how could we even say something against mysticism? You understand why this is impossible? If a mystic says that that sort of experience exists, what could we say but that it does not exist, that it is a sort of illusion? And that, finally, would not even be a very strong argument. And so, does such an experience exist? Does there exist such a movement on a purely individual level, as something like a purely personal event? Maybe. Finally, there is nothing more that philosophy can say on this point.

And so there are only two enemies of philosophy – positivism and nihilism – because we cannot exactly say that mysticism is an enemy of philosophy. In some sense, both affirm the same: first there is an experience, a necessary experience of nothingness, and second there exists a possibility of going beyond nothingness. There is, however, something in philosophy which is more on the side of patience, construction, conceptualization, labor, and so on – the movement is not pure and immediate. And it is strange, very strange to imagine a society of mystics, a society where everyone is a mystic, where everyone is completely captured in God. Such a society would be a dissolution of collectivity, a dissolution of all collectivity, of all positive collectivity. It's a strange image, an image of science fiction in fact: a society where there is pure juxtaposition of all individuals individually with God, a society where all individuals are an in immediate and exclusive relationship with God. Maybe this would be the situation of angels – if angels exist? As you know, in Medieval philosophy's descriptions of angels, the angel is in such an intimate relationship with God that all which is not God does not exist for the angel, in some sense. In fact, the most complete angels – in the tradition of Aristotle, maybe there could be a classification of angels: poor angels, very aristocratic angels, and so on – the purest angels would be in a constant mysticism, a constant and immediate relationship with the infinite, a constant experimentation of the love of God for the angel, and, consequently, there would be a complete disparition of everything which is not of that sort of experience. And so, maybe a society of mystics would be something like a society of angels. The difference, in some sense, between philosophy and mysticism is that philosophy says that we are not angels.... Maybe some of us are angels... why not? Hidden angels, angels disguised as human beings.... But, finally, for philosophy it is very important to confirm that we are not angels, and so that mysticism is not an obligatory destiny, that it is not our destiny.

To distinguish philosophy from mysticism we must, therefore, affirm that the construction of the philosophical movement is always systematic. Today – as we all know – to say that something is systematic is to depreciate that thing. And this is especially the case for philosophy. But it really is an absolute criteria of philosophy: philosophy is systematic, and so the end of systems would be the end of philosophy. Finally, to say that something is systematic does mean that it is in the image of a machine, or that there is no freedom, it means only that we have a construction, it's only this: we have a definition of some steps, and we have a description of the movement.

A system, then, is something like a consciousness of the existence of different steps in the movement from negativity to affirmation – it simply affirms that the movement is not an immediate revelation, but that we have to learn, that we have to understand, that we have to have a sort of patience, that there exist some moments of repetition, and finally, that all of this is rational and transmissible. And across the history of philosophy we have many different systems, many different possibilities of constructing this movement. Each philosophy, in fact, proposes a particular construction of this passage, a particular systematic construction of the passage from nothingness to affirmation, from zero to one, from the void to the infinite.

The clearest example of such a construction is a number line, which is a simple inscription of the movement from zero to the infinite.

$$0, 1, 2, 3, 4, 5, \ldots n, n+1, \ldots \omega$$

As you can see, the number line is also a form of repetition moving towards the infinite. As you all know, there is no last number, there is no final number, and so the succession on numbers is infinite. This line is for us a sort of image of the passage from nothingness – 0 is the numerical name for nothingness – to something beyond all numbers, to the first infinite. As you can see the passage from 1 to 2, to 3, and so on, is a repetition. It is a repetition because we repeat the same operation, the same process, and this process is the passage from n to $n+1$. Each step is, therefore, a repetition of the step before. The question that we must ask is: is the philosophical passage of the same nature as the numerical succession?

This scheme is not a philosophical one, but an arithmetical one. It is an image for the philosopher, it's only an image, an image of the passage from zero in direction to the infinite. But this image is interesting on two points. First, the passage contains a repetition, not a repetition of the object, but the repetition of the passage from one object to another object. You know that, for example, 3 is not the same number as 2, so it is not the repetition of the object – the sequence is not 1, 1, 1, 1... and so on. There is really something new with each repetition: the number 3 is not the number 2, and so repetition is something like a new number. What repeats is not the result, the construction, but the operation of the construction. Philosophically, what we have is a process of the production of difference and not a process of pure repetition of the same object. This image represents the possibility of creating something new inside, or by the means of repetition: the passage from 2 to 3 is, in some sense, a pure repetition of the passage from 1 to 2, and so on, it is exactly the same operation, and yet the result is not the same, because 3 is not 2, and 2 not equal to 1, and so on. We produce, therefore, something new by the repetition of the same operation. This is, in fact, a very simple dialectics of difference and identity: we have difference, the production of difference – infinitely different numbers – by the means of repetition, by the means of something which is not at all different but absolutely identical. This is an image of this dialectics, it an image of what finds its most achieved philosophical determination in the philosophy of Hegel – Hegel's philosophy is entirely the extraordinary construction of something new with the dialectic of identity and difference. Finally, we can say that the number, which is purely arithmetical, is, in some sense, dialectical. And so, the most elementary and most clear object of mathematics is not purely analytical but dialectical. This is the first point. And this first point is very important: if philosophy must go beyond nihilism – not in the mystic form, but in the form of a real process – it will be by a process which is a mixture, a dialectical mixture, of identity and difference.

Today, as you know, the question of identity and differences is at the very center of the ideological fight: the fundamental question of politics today is the question of identity, of respect for differences, of the Derridean concept of *différance*, and so on. We must come to understand that dialectics is not at all an old and dogmatic question, we must affirm that the question of dialectics, the possibility of dialectics, is of fundamental importance today. And, in some sense, we find the essence of all that in the simple succession of numbers. It is just an image, a very simple but also very clear image, of something very complex and very difficult, but it is also the image of something very important today, of something very important politically. After all, if there is something which is political today, it is the problem of the relationship between identity and difference – we have, for example, the question of gender, the question of different cultures, of minorities, of immigration, and finally, of the excluded. And all of those questions are so many forms of a problem that can be abstractly presented in the succession of numbers.

You all know perfectly well that in the relationship with the other, the question is simultaneously the difference from the other and the identity with the other. And we must ask: what is more important, difference or identity? This is absolutely a political question, and, in fact, a question which is a constant difficulty. Ultimately we must affirm, *we must absolutely affirm*, that it is identity, and yet we must make this affirmation in a way that respects and accepts all difference. But we must decide which is more important. After all, if identity is more important than difference the consequences are not at all the same as if we were to affirm that difference is more important than identity. Even in our image we find this choice, and, ultimately, this contradiction: we can say 'all the numbers are absolutely different, 3 is completely different from 2', or we can say 'yes, but 3 comes from 2 by exactly the same operation as 2 came from 1'. And so, even in this simple image, in the identity of the process and the difference of the result we have a real dialectical contradiction.

The second point which we can find in this image, is that this term 'omega' (ω) does not result from repetition: omega as such is not the result of a sequence operated by something like n+1. If we take a number – as big as you want – this number +1 is another number. This sequence, therefore, can never succeed in reaching the infinite. Certainly, the process goes in the direction of omega, but it can never produce omega. The infinite cannot be produced by this process because it can never reach the infinite as such. Why? Because the number that succeeds the first number is itself a finite number – which can itself be succeeded – and not an infinite number. This is the second point: this process is a process from zero *towards the infinite*, but the infinite as such is not the result of the process. Therefore, there must be a cut here – between n+1 and ω – there must be something like an interruption of this process oriented towards the infinite but never capable of reaching the infinite.

$$0, 1, 2, 3, 4, \ldots n, n+1, \ldots \mid \omega$$

The totality of the process – from 0 to ω – is, therefore, constituted not only by the repeated passage from one number to the next, but also by some interruption of this repetition. Repetition as such has no end – after every number we can produce, by the operator of succession, another number – and so the infinite can only be on the other side of this repetition. And so, if the philosophical process is really the passage from pure negativity to an absolute affirmation – like with the succession of numbers – we must affirm that there is not only one operation, but two completely different operations.

The first operation is a repetitive one. And there is in every philosophy a repetitive operation, an operation which is always of the same form. We can immediately give many examples: in the Hegelian dialectic, in the Kantian critique, in the metaphysics of Descartes, or Leibniz, you can very easily identify some operations which are constantly repeated by the philosopher, some passage form one notion to another notion, which creates a new concept. Naturally, the repeated operation is very important in any philosophy, and in philosophy in general. In Descartes, for example, it's the deductive passage of one sentence to another sentence, with a mathematical method. For Hegel, on the other hand, it is the dialectical passage by negativity from one assertion to another assertion.

But there is another operation, which is the operation of a cut, of an interruption of repetition. We must assume also this second form of operation, which is a rupture *inside* repetition, an interruption *of* repetition. The image of that is clearly the position of the first infinite number, which is omega (ω), in regard to all the other numbers, all the finite numbers. Repetition certainly goes in the direction of the last term, which is the first infinite number. But there is no possibility of reaching this term by the strict action of the repetitive operation. And so, if you affirm the existence of omega, you must create a cut in repetition, a cut with repetition. Omega, we can say, is the beyond of repetition – in mathematics, in fact, is it said that omega is the limit of repetition.

And so, in philosophy – where the question is to go from the experience of negativity to an absolute affirmation, but not in a mystical way, not in an immediate way – we must consider two absolutely different operations. This duality is a fundamental aspect of philosophy, because there is always a moment in philosophy where we cannot only continue the fundamental operation. In Plato this is very clear. The fundamental operation is – as you know – the dialectic discussion. And these discussions involve arguments, sometimes opposed arguments, which propose successive definitions of something. For example, we have a discussion about the question of the very essence of courage, and in this discussion there is a sequence of

successive refutations of opposed arguments until the definition
of the thing in question is reached, until – in this instance –the
definition of courage is found. The dialectical discussion is
certainly the fundamental operation in the philosophy of Plato.
But, finally, we cannot go forth only in the form of discussion.
And so, Plato creates something completely different, which is a
myth, a poetic myth, or a story, the story of Err at the end of
Republic, for example. And these images are exactly in the
position of the cut.

The dialectical discussion is the successive production of many
possibilities of definitions, new concepts, and so on, but at the
end, when you are at the question of the absolute, we cannot go
further by this same operation, and it is why Plato proposes
something like an image. A characteristic, absolutely
characteristic text is when Plato proposes the conception of the
Idea of the Good at the end of the discussion, and he explicitly
says that he cannot propose a pure concept, a pure definition of
this Idea, but only an image, and it's the image of the sun – he
says that the Idea is, in regard to all the concepts, in the same
position as the sun is in regard to life, in regard to the world.

But why is it just an image? Why can we not continue? Precisely
because there is a moment where, *by necessity*, there is an
operation which is in the form of a cut, an interruption, and not a
continuation of the dialectical discussion. And so the presence of
myths in Plato is not at all an idiosyncrasy of some dialogue, it is
not at all something strange but precisely the second operation,
the second operation after the rational creation of concepts by
means of rational discussion. And it is always like this in Plato
and across all philosophy, in fact. And to find the two distinct
operations in the philosophical system is another possible way to
read the great philosophers. In every philosophical system there
is always a moment where the fundamental operation of the
philosopher is no longer useful and must be replaced with

something else – in Plato, we know, this is the myth, which is proposed after a long sequence of rational discussions. We find two such operations in absolutely every philosopher. And maybe – if the system is very complex – we find three or four operations.

This is why my most important concepts – I speak of myself, for a moment – are precisely of the same form. As you know, my question is to find something that is the dialectical result of universality and particularity, something like the singularity in Hegel. But the question is: by what sorts of operations can we arrive at something like that? When I propose that truth is the name for that sort of exception, that sort of immanent exception, which is simultaneously of particular nature and addressed to everybody, with the possibility of resurrection in another world, the question is: what sorts of operations are necessary for the construction of such a truth? Certainly, therefore, I must propose a name for creative repetition, like the passage from 1 to 2 – I say creative repetition because there is a repetition of the passage, of the operation, and yet the results are new, and so it is, strictly speaking, a creative repetition, I do the same thing, but the result is different. I must propose something like that, but I must also propose something that describes the cut, the second operation. The name I propose for the cut, for the second operation, is the concept of event: an event is precisely in the position of the interruption of repetition. And for the first operation I propose the concept fidelity: fidelity is the name for creative repetition. The uniqueness of my position is, ultimately, that – and here we have the difference with arithmetical image – before 0 there is a cut as well. Why? Because it is a question of the beginning, and the beginning cannot be the result of repetition.

We have said that at the beginning there is an experience, a pure experience of negativity, and we must understand that if that sort of experience happens it cannot be the result of repetition – it is a cut, it is a cut in our lives. When, at some moment, you have such an experience – a true experience of anxiety, of nothingness, of nihilism – it is something which is not a repetition of our normal lives, but something which happens, and which is, very often, not so pleasant. The name of this moment is event, and it is something which is precisely an interruption of our lives, of the world as it is, in some sense. The process of the construction of a truth, therefore, begins by an event. The entire sequence is then something like this:

event ——————————————————⟶ truth

The process is a movement from an event to a truth. And so, it is not exactly like the arithmetical image, but something different. However, there is something like omega in the concept of truth, and something like zero in the concept of event. There is, then, an interruption at the beginning and at the end. *We must understand that if truths exist, and if they are immanent exceptions, then there must always be these two types of operations, the second of which is at the beginning and at the end*! There must be an interruption at the beginning because a beginning cannot be the result of repetition, if it were it would not be a beginning but a continuation! In my philosophical system there are two interruptions – one as the beginning, and one as the end – the names of which are event and truth, and between them we have the operation of fidelity, which is, naturally, fidelity to an event, fidelity to some interruption. To finish, I will propose a succession of concepts:

existence $\neq$ being	event	fidelity	subject	truth

We have here a succession of concepts, which is a recapitulation of what we have said. First we have being and existence, the dialectical contradiction between being and existence. And this is a question of ontology. An event, in some sense, is always a rupture inside the question of the relationship between being and existence. It opens a new possibility, and, in some sense, it is like the cut that creates the possibility of an infinite number beyond the succession of finite numbers. An event is, ultimately, what opens a new possibility. In some sense it is exactly like the cut that creates the possibility of the infinite beyond all finite numbers, but more generally it is always something which creates the possibility of a rupture in a certain form of the relationship between being and existence, and in this way creates a new possibility.

Fidelity is the organization of the consequences of the event, and so, it is something like creative repetition. In fact, this is precisely the definition of fidelity in the field of love: love is not reducible to not having a sexual relationship with another person, it is a construction, the construction of a love. And so it is the continuation of something, but a continuation which cannot continue by strict repetition, it is a continuation which must be creative. As all of us know, to continue by strict repetition is impossible: the problem of love is how to continue and not to repeat, how to invent something new inside the continuation of a love. In love, the event is the amorous encounter – when you encounter someone it is, maybe, the beginning of a love. But, after that, we must construct something, we must create something. And this process is, in some sense, a repetition – I continue with the same person – but in another sense it is a construction, an invention. This process is a creative repetition, it is a fidelity.

Inside of fidelity – and in order to orient a fidelity – we must, by necessity, have a new subject. And this subject, naturally, will be determined by the particular event in the initial situation of the relationship between being and existence. The subject is the operator of fidelity. This sequence of concepts is what creates a truth – a true love, a truth in science, an artistic truth, and so on.

Within this sequence there is something that is appropriate to each of these fields. To think the event, we have art. It is not philosophy which allows us to think what exactly an event is, but art – philosophy creates the concept of event, and develops its formal characteristics, but if we want to describe a particular event it is always art which is the strongest possibility. And this is why mysticism – which is the reduction of the entire process to a single moment, to the event alone – is always expressed in poetic form, it is always expressed by art. Fidelity, on the other hand, we find in logic, which is an abstract theory of creative repetition. But, much more generally, logic is a theory of consequences, and as a theory of consequences it is, finally, an abstract representation of fidelity, of the same operation which when repeated creates something new. The classical field for the subject is psychology, if we speak of the individual subject, and politics, if we speak of a collective subject. And, finally, the theoretical field of truth is epistemology, which describes the conditions of a truth, of what is a truth, what is a scientific truth, and so on.

existence | event | fidelity | subject | truth
$\neq$
being

↑ (being)   ↑ (event)   ↑ (fidelity)   ↑ (subject)   ↑ (truth)

ontology   art   logic   epistemology

politics/psychology

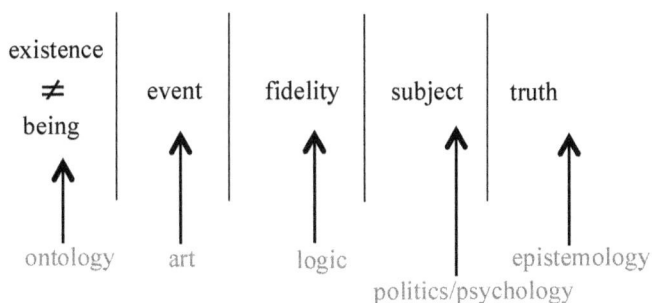

I can now conclude. The beginning of a process of truth is in the relationship of being and existence, and that is a question of ontology. How else can we begin, after all, but by what exists, by what is? We always begin with the world as it is, in its being and its existence. After that – in order to open the possibility of something new – we have a rupture with repetition, and so we have the event. And to construct something on the basis of this rupture must have some form of creative repetition, which is a fidelity to an event. Once more, let me say that love is probably the clearest example of this. All of this, it is true, constructs a new subject, a new individual or a new collective subject of the event. For example, love construct a new subject which is not a one + one, but a Two, and this Two is the new subject because it does not exist before the encounter, and it does not exist before fidelity. And, finally, a truth is something affirmative in the construction of event-fidelity-subject, and which is a possibility for everyone. In fact – as we have said – a truth can be resurrected in another world. And so, it is something which can be understood and continued in a completely different world, and this is as true of love as it is of mathematics, art or politics. As philosophers, what we must affirm is that philosophy can explain all of that: philosophy is always the affirmation that something like the process of a truth exists and that it can be understood by rational means.

Philosophy is the general thinking of this movement: it is the thought of its constitution by two distinct operations – interruption and creative repetition – and of it's sequence of moments – existence-being, event, fidelity, subject, and truth. We can now, finally, affirm that these moments cannot be studied separately, at least, not as philosophy. And if they are studied separately, then it is not properly philosophy but scholasticism that is at stake. To separate this sequence, this process, into ontology, aesthetics, logic, politics, and so on, to separate these moments from one another, is, finally, to reduce philosophy to the discourse of the university. But, philosophy is not exactly the addition of these moments, or their proper fields – it is not a little logic, a little epistemology, a little politics, a little art, and so on. No! Philosophy is the understanding of the complete path, of the complete process of a truth. And so, naturally, in every great philosophy we find ontology, aesthetics, logic, politics, and so on, but this is not the same as to say that philosophy is the pure sum of these elements. No! Philosophy is the movement, the integral movement, of the construction of a truth. And so, we cannot affirm that there are different pieces which can be put together, because there is only the construction of the process, and this process is constructed in such a way that it is rational and universally transmissible.

This point is profound: I am not saying something directly against this academic disposition, after all, maybe it would be interesting to have some notions concerning the different parts independently, *but it would not be philosophy*! And this is precisely why we cannot divide the great philosophers – Plato, Aristotle, Kant, Heidegger, Deleuze and so on – into separate parts, we cannot cut them into pieces. We know that there exists something like the philosophy of Deleuze, but its not ontology, and aesthetics, and politics, and so on. No! It is the philosophy of Deleuze! And it's also a style, a form of writing, a feeling, and, finally, it is something that goes from an existential experience to the creation of concepts, without being a decomposition of the process into pieces. Philosophy, finally, is a single thing, there is a unity of the philosophical construction! And, in this sense, it is very much like a work of art, because it is not a collection of different disciplines, techniques, colors and so on, *a work of art is a creation of something*, and its the same in philosophy. Philosophy, finally, is much more like a work of art than something like an academic learning.

Thank you.

4. Day Four

4.1 Lecture VII

There will be three parts to this afternoon. First, the end of something concerning the philosophical conceptual process – with existence, being, event, fidelity, subject, truth and so on. Second, a lecture, by me, of a text – not the text you have, but another text, which you will have as well. And, after that, a discussion of your questions.

This morning we said that the philosophical process – which is a process with different steps, different conceptual constructions and so on, and which is not an immediate intuition of the infinite, as in mystical experience – begins by something of ontological nature – existence, being – and that at the end we have truth, and that within this process we also have event, fidelity and subject. All of this, naturally, can be different, in the sense of a different language, with different conception, different invention, and so on. And, sometimes there is a change of order or a change of accent. But, finally, we find all of this in every philosophical system. This sequence of concepts, this sequence of constructions – being, existence, event, fidelity, subject and truth – is the philosophical process in my proper language.

I can explain two differences, two details. First, the beginning is something ontological, that is, it is something concerning being and existence, or the two concepts in their relation. We can say that the beginning is in a situation, and, in fact, all processes begin in a situation, in a concrete situation. But a situation can be thought from the point of view of being or from the point of view of existence. At the beginning, therefore, there is a

138

concrete situation, but at the philosophical level situation has two possible meanings: first, a purely ontological one, and so situation in the broad sense, or second, the situation from the point of view of appearance, from the point of view of what really exists in the situation. We have already seen that this is precisely the dialectical nature of philosophy – philosophy always thinks the difference between being and existence.

All of this is to say that for philosophy there are two different possible interpretations, two different analyses – two different philosophical analyses – of the sequence of ontology, event, fidelity, subject, and, finally, truth. There are two different ways to think all of that: first from the point of view of being as such, and so the situation is thought in its being, or second, from the point of view of existence, that is, from the point of view of appearance, from the point of view of what exists, of what appears in the world.

We find a clear example of this difference in Hegel: in Hegel we have two great books, *The Phenomenology* and *The Logic*. It is clear: *The Logic* is the question of truth from the point of view of being as such, and so Hegel begins the *Logic* with the completely void concept of being as such – we begin with being. The *Phenomenology* – the other great book of Hegel – is from the point of view of existence, and from the point of view of consciousness – it's the other possibility. And the two books are not at all in contradiction – they are just two different interpretations of the construction of the truth: first from the point of view of pure being, and second from the point of view of historical existence, from the specificity of a world, from the history of consciousness. This distinction is very general and we find it across the entire history of philosophy. For example, in Plato we can find the same division: a book like *Parmenides* is from the point of view of being, absolutely, but a book like *The Apology*, for example, is form the point of view of concrete existence. *But the question is the same*! The question is not at all a different question... it is always the question of immanent exception, and so the question of truth.

And so the distinction between pure being and appearance, or being and existence, is also a methodological difference in philosophy. It is not only an ontological difference, naturally, but also a difference in the writing of philosophy. The two are the two forms of writing philosophy. When you write from existence very often your writing – your style – is not the same as if you were to begin from pure being. In general, we can say that when a philosopher begins by pure being the writing is very logical, very strict, and very near mathematics, while if the philosopher begins on the side of the concrete world, on the side of existence or consciousness, the writing will be much more like a novel, like a philosophical novel, like the story of truth in a concrete world. And this distinction is not a contradiction, not at all. It creates – probably across the entire history of philosophy – two tendencies, two obscure tendencies, two styles of writing philosophy. We have philosophers who prefer to begin with the concrete world, with existence, and so on, and we can name them existentialists, in some sense. And so existentialists exist from the very beginning of philosophy. The other tendency, which prefers to begin with pure being, we can name essentialist – and so we have something like existentialists against essentialists from the very beginning. But, finally, every great philosopher is both – sometimes there is an exception, sometimes.

In Heidegger this is the distinction between... being and being... between *être* and *étant* – the English language is not an ontological language! The great English philosophical tradition is empiricism, and it's a great creation, a very important concept – it's the creation of Hume, and Locke, and so on. But in empiricism the idea is that we have to affirm that there is no difference between existence and being, that what we see, that what exists in the world is really what exists absolutely, and that there is nothing other than what appears. Finally, empiricism is the idea that all that exists is our experience: everything of which we have experience exists and also is, and only that is and exists. But in every great attempt to be rigorously empiricist we recognize something at the end, which is of ontological nature. And why? Because it's impossible to develop a consistent philosophy which is strictly empiricist, it's impossible. But the idea is *that there is no difference, that there is no difference between being and existence.* And it is why sometimes we cannot translate a philosophical notion into English. Some French distinctions, for example on the side of subjectivity, begin by the subject, but it is a French word and not an English word – the English word is 'self', and it is not at all the same thing as subject. On the side of ontological philosophy – German philosophy – the difficulty of translating philosophy into English concerns ontological concepts. And so the distinction with what exists... between to exist and to be is very difficult to understand in its complete consequences in English. When we must translate the German present participle of being and the infinitive to be we cannot translate it fully into English, its impossible. And so, generally, the solution is to name being with a big 'B' and what exists with a small 'b'.

So you see, language is always a symptom, because on the side of 'to be' we have a big 'B', and so there is a condition in language for something more majestic, something more important. But the tendency in empiricism is to say that this very majestic, great Being is, in fact, nothing at all... that Being is nothing at all. And so, we must be content with the small 'b', which is, finally, what exists and all that is. As you all know, all of that is the history of what Heidegger named ontological difference. For Heidegger, in fact, the entire history of philosophy is the history of ontological difference. And the history of that sort of distance – between to be and to exist – is a central concept in the philosophy of Heidegger explicitly, but it is, ultimately, also a central concept in every philosophy. And Heidegger is a great historian of philosophy precisely because his interpretation of the entire history of philosophy is really consistent with that distinction, with that sort of consistent vision of the ontological difference between to be and to exist.

And so for philosophy there is not only one sequence of concepts from ontology to epistemology – from ontology to the question of truth, from the question of being to the question of truth – but two possible interpretations of this sequence – the purely ontological interpretation, and the interpretation that begins much more with appearance and existence. Sometimes this distinction is named in the form of the opposition of dogmatic philosophy, which is a philosophy of being, and empiricist philosophy, which is exactly the philosophy of existence. But – I repeat – every attempt to construct a philosophical system is always a mixture of the two interpretations. It is simply that sometimes the beginning is much more on the side of empiricism, and sometimes the beginning is much more on the side of ontology. But, finally, we can always interpret a philosophy as an interdependency between the two possibilities.

And, finally, this is why a lecture, or a reading of philosophy, is practically always divided, and why it's difficult to completely unify a lecture, a reading, an interpretation.... Philosophy is difficult not only because of the tension between particularity and universality, or because we have the question of the nihilist experience of nothingness and after that the construction of affirmation, or even because philosophy is something which is impure in its language, but also because there are two possible beginnings for philosophy. There are two possible beginnings in any treatise of philosophy, or any philosophical construction, and so we always have the question of the relationship between the two, and also the reason for the choice of one beginning rather than the other – and all that is, finally, a subjective choice. And it is *because it is a subjective choice* that we find both beginnings across the entire history of philosophy. There is no historical passage from the one beginning to the other. No! It really is a subjective choice, a subjective choice between the two beginnings.

What is the nature of this choice? When a philosopher, and finally everybody – everybody who reads philosophy – prefers one over the other, we must ask what the cause of this preference is. I think that the grounds for this choice are the different possible manners of confronting the primitive experience of nihilism. That is the point. The cause is this relationship to nothingness... because the experience of nihilism, of nothingness, is purely a subjective one. It's an experience, it's really an experience, and not at all something which is of a conceptual nature. And so the difference of subjectivity is also the difference in the nature of this experience, which is, finally, an experience of anxiety. We can absolutely recognize that sort of experience in the style of the philosopher. Sometimes it is a terrible experience, and the philosophy is then also something like a means to escape this experience. The experience is a necessity, certainly, but if the experience is a terrible thing, then we have the desire to escape quickly, we have the desire to not stay in nihilism. If you read the circumstances of the life of the philosopher, there is always something like that. Generally that sort of experience prefers the beginning on the side of being, because existence is completely on the side of anxiety. And so that sort of philosophy is a movement that desires to go completely beyond the primitive experience of negativity to some affirmation, and to do so as quickly as possible. But there is also a form of philosophy where, on the contrary, the experience of negativity is a temptation, and, in fact, something like a measure of the potency of life. In such a case the experience is something like an experience of the limit of life. And so, it is a temptation, and the philosopher then does not go beyond that sort of experience quickly, but dwells in the experience, he dwells on the description of that experience, on the consequences of experience. This experience – the very nature of this experience – then assumes a large place in the philosophical disposition. Why? Precisely because it is not just a point to be moved beyond.

I return to the example of Descartes, since Descartes is typical of the first tendency. In Descartes we have a very precise description of the negative character of the duped, of the possibility of complete nihilism, of a complete destruction of all possible knowledge. But Descartes moves very quickly to the first affirmation – which is precisely the affirmation of the pure being of subjectivity. But if you read Nietzsche, or Kierkegaard, on the other hand, you find a very long description of the experience of negativity, and a great importance placed on this existential experience of negativity. And in Schopenhauer, for example, you find an entire philosophy that develops the description of anxiety, suffering, and so on, as a very long and important part of the philosophical disposition as such. And so – to return to our question – the choice between the two possible beginnings, the two necessary and possible sites of philosophy – the site of being and the site of existence – is really of biographical nature. It really is a purely subjective choice. As you all know, Nietzsche has written that philosophy is the biography of the philosopher: it is a philosophy, with concepts and so on, but, ultimately, it's also the story of the life of the philosopher. As so often in Nietzsche, it's not absolutely true but it's not absolutely false either.... It's not absolutely false because there really are some subjective, some biographical elements in conceptual philosophy, and we must accept that sort of immersion.

And so it is impossible to reduce the figure of the philosopher to the figure of the scientist, for example. Certainly the goal in each case is to find something universal, but in a scientific result the life of the scientist disappears. We can know that Einstein did this and that, but, finally, the lives of great scientists are not in the result: the result is the book, the theorem, the laws of physics and so on, and all biographical elements disappear. The figure of the scientist is the figure of the disparition of subjectivity. It is not wanting of subjectivity – there is a concrete situation and a concrete scientist – but the work itself organizes the disparition of subjectivity. In philosophy, on the other hand, this is impossible. In philosophy the subjectivity of the philosopher cannot completely disappear. And so – in some sense – it is true that there is always something biographical in a philosophy. And, I propose the most important symptom of this is the choice of the beginning – the choice of beginning on the side of existence, or beginning on the side of being. This choice is the most important symptom of the very subjective nature of philosophy.

Now, maybe, I can return to my case.... As you know, I have written two big books of philosophy: the first is *Being and Event*, and the second is *Logics of Worlds*. You can see by their titles that the first one is on the side of being and the second on the side of appearance, or existence. I can say something about how – from my proper experience – I see the difference, the difference between the two books. After all, if there is always something biographical in a philosophy, allow me to expose some biographical remarks concerning the difference of the two books, by some subjective indications. The first book is really under the question of what exactly is the possible understanding of the being of truths, the question is: what is the being of truth, if a truth is something like an immanent exception? *Being and Event* is clearly the question of what is a truth from the position of being. And so, when I was writing this book the great question was the order of concepts, it was a question of what I can name constructive subjectivity. And why? Why is the question of the order of concepts the first question? Because truth comes at the end of the process of being-event-fidelity-subject-truth, and so, to understand what is the being of truth you most to go from a conception of being to a conception of truth with the same question, that is, with the question of being itself. And so, it was necessary to explore the question of being as such: it was necessary to ask what the being of an event is, what the being of fidelity is, what the being of a subject is, and, finally, what the being of truth is. *The question of order was absolutely essential.* It was absolutely essential because if we do not respect the order of concepts, then something of the very nature of the question disappears, and what disappears, in fact, is precisely the question of being! If we do not respect the order, then we find ourselves not in the question of being but in the question of the existence of truth – the historical existence of a truth by a subject, after a fidelity, in consequence of event, and so on. And it was a very complex question, because, in general, the question of the being of truth is not an immanent question.

In classical metaphysics – and in a big part of the history of philosophy in general, and in Heidegger too – the question of the being of truth is not exactly the question of its being, but very often the question of its existence. For example, it is clear that the great debate between skepticism and dogmatism in philosophy has been over the existence of truth – is it possible to know something like a truth, or is it possible to know *the* truth, and so on. In such a debate we have a certain conception of truth, *but the question is not over its being, but over our capacity to know it* – it is a debate over *the possibility and impossibility of knowing the truth, and not over what it is*. And such a discussion concerns the existence of a truth – it is not a discussion of its being. Again, we find here another example of the distance between to be and to exist.

There is another side to this choice, which is in relation to the context of the 1980's – this book was written in '88: in the context of the 80's the question of truth was always reduced to a linguistic question. This was the dominant current. The question was: is it possible for a proposition of a language to be true? Or: what is the correct language to produce sentences which are true? And so on. And so the question of truth was the question of the truth of a proposition, of the truth of a judgment. My vision of what a truth is, on the other hand, was not at all that sort of vision. For me a truth can be a work of art, a political revolution, a scientific theory, and so on, and a great love too, and it's not reducible to the strict question of the truth of a judgment. My question is not: what am I saying when I say the snow is white? That is an analytic question, a typical analytic question. Nor is my question: why the judgment 'the snow is white' is true? Nor even: what I am saying when I say that the judgment, or sentence, 'the snow is white is' true? And so on. But this was absolutely the context – it was the dominant philosophical disposition of that time. The dominant context was the reduction of the question of truth not to the question what is a universal creation in culture, but to the question of judgment, the question of the sentence, of the proposition. At this time, truth was a linguistic question, absolutely, and not at all an ontological one – the question of truth was not at all the question of the being of a truth, but the question of what is a correct proposition, a correct sentence. And so, I wrote *Being and Event* in a completely different position than the dominant one.

In that sort of context it was an obligation for me to be extremely strict in the order of the book, and so in its construction, and to give the book the form of something like a big proof, *a big proof*. It was necessary to give a big proof, a big demonstration first of my definition of truth, and then a proof of this conception. Given the dominant context, the book was also in opposition to – in a fight against – the reduction of truth to purely linguistic criteria. And this is why this book has two subjective characteristics: first, it is a book where the order is a constructive order, and second, it is also a book that fights against the dominant position, against the position that was victorious in France during those years. The academy was absolutely dominated by the analytic point of view. It was – if you like – the Americanization of France. You know France is always 20 years behind America? Even in this sense, because in America purely analytic philosophy was largely finished when it was victorious in France. It was paradoxical situation, and so – in some sense – I was like Don Quixote, fighting against the windmill. But that was the situation – my situation – and so *Being and Event* is a book of a very strict nature, and a book in which I was also saying to my enemies that on the side of logic and mathematics I was perfect. And this was absolutely a part of the demonstration, because, in general, they were saying 'wait, wait, wait, you don't know anything about mathematics, and this is why you don't adopt the analytic point of view.' Logic and the mathematics of logic were absolutely on the side of the analytical point of view in the field of philosophy. And so *Being and Event* was a demonstration to say that we could know logic, mathematics, mathematizable logic perfectly *and still affirm something completely contradictory to the analytic position*! This book, in this way, posed a great problem for many years for the analytic point of view, because – generally speaking – before it, it was possible to say 'okay, okay, but French philosophy is something on the side of literature, interpretations, hermeneutics, it is something aesthetic, and so on, but it does not know the serious questions, the questions of science, of mathematics, the questions of logic, and so on', but after it, this was no longer possible.

So you see... philosophy is also always in a context, and its always in a context of contradiction, in a fight, in a difficulty, and the subjectivity, the philosophical subjectivity, is also a fighting subjectivity, and not at all a peaceful one. And so, Kant was right: philosophy is a battlefield! We are beginning to see why! It is because there are tendencies, positions, dialectical constructions, oppositions, and so on. It is a necessity! The subjectivity of *Being and Event*, then, was a contradictory subjectivity: on one hand it was order, mathematics, pure construction, demonstration, and all that, and on the other hand it was a fighting subjectivity against the apparent victory of the analytic tendency in the academic context of France in the 1980s. Naturally, the result is a book that is cold, very cold – it is a book in the form of a perfect construction with mathematics, exactly in the place where mathematics must be.

And you know the book was completely ignored when it was finished – it was a complete failure, a complete failure in France, but also in other countries. The first recognition of the book was in the States – I must say this. And this was a strange situation for me, because it then became necessary for me to love America. And so I recognize my debt to you, and to others, because in France it was a real failure. But it was a failure for one simple reason: it was a failure because it was impossible for the enemies to say anything concerning this book – it was impossible because the book was perfect, in some sense. It was perfect not because it was true, but because it was formally perfect – it was impossible to say 'Badiou does not know anything concerning logic, mathematics', this was impossible. And, in general, I know much more than the enemies concerning that sort of thing. The good solution, the only possible solution, was to say nothing. And this was precisely the result: there was a complete silence concerning the book. And maybe this result was the mark of a strategic failure, because in philosophy too there is strategy, after all. And so the first book was in something like a strange time, a strange time for it, naturally.

The second book is completely different. The second book was written after the first had been recognized, and so it was not written within the failure of the first appearance of *Being and Event*. It was a completely different context, and so I could write *Logics of Worlds* in a completely different subjectivity, a subjectivity which was much more free, much more anarchic.

I want to tell you now a short story. At the beginning of the new century – ten years after the first book – I had, naturally, the idea, the general idea, of the second book. I perfectly knew that the second book had to be a book from the point of view of existence, and not from the point of view of being. It was not my *Logic* – like *Being and Event* – but my *Phenomenology* – to be Hegelian. And it is a book from the point of view of existence. And so, the question was not the being of truth, but how a truth appears in a world: *Logics of Worlds* assumes the problem of the concrete appearance of a truth in a world. This is why one of its main concepts is the body, the body of a truth, the material existence of a truth in a concrete world. If in a world all is bodies, we must, then, have something like the concrete body of a truth. The truth must also be in a form of objectivity, not by itself, naturally, but if a truth exists in a world of objects, then it must have a body. Truth does not exist in some other, transcendental world – in the sky, and so on – truth must exist *here, concretely, in this world*. This was my question, and so – in some sense – it was a completely different question than the question of *Being and Event*.

When I began *Logics of Worlds* I had a strict order in mind, but it was completely false – I was trying to repeat *Being and Event* – and so it was impossible to write the book. The order was the same – existence, event, fidelity, subject, truth. And I was in complete despair because it was impossible to write the book, because the book was not good, and so on. During practically an entire year while I was trying to write the book I was in a crisis, a real crisis. And it was a philosophical crisis, because I was confronting the idea that maybe it was impossible to write concerning truth from the point of view of existence. It was a great difficulty, and a great problem, because if it is impossible to write concerning truth from the point of view of existence, then truth is something that does not exist, that cannot exist. And so, if truth is it could only exist in another world, and so, *by necessity*, we would have something like a religious solution, a transcendent solution, a solution where truth is outside of the world. And so, it was a crisis of my fundamental materialism, because if truth cannot exist in a world and if I am materialist, then I must conclude that truth does not exist at all... or I must conclude that truth exists in the sky of idealism, and so I would be a dualist, and must recognize the existence of something like a God. It was a profound crisis: it was a crisis between my materialist subjectivity and the serious question of truth from the double point of view of the being of truth and the existence of truth.

And, now – finally – my little story. The possibility of going beyond this crisis – of passing through it – was made possible by a pure experience. I think, in fact, by something that is near a mystic experience. I was in New York, and New York was absolutely white, it was completely under snow, and there was a complete silence in the city. The city was all white and in complete silence, and I was alone, absolutely alone. And, finally, I was also in complete despair because it was impossible to write the second book. And then, suddenly, I had the vision of the book – it's true, it's really true, I had a vision of the book. And at once I understood that the construction of the book cannot at all be the construction of *Being and Event*, and that I had been in a false subjectivity, and that I must transform my subjectivity. For example, in order to explain the possibility of the existence of a truth – of the appearance of a truth – in a world I had to be much more in different examples, much more in a sort of disorder – or in an appearance of disorder – and, finally – and much more importantly – I had to begin with the question of the subject, and not finish with the question of the subject, like in *Being and Event*. It was suddenly clear that the existence of the subject must be affirmed at the beginning of the book and not at the end. And, naturally so, since, if the point of departure is existence then it must be a subjective point of departure. It was sudden, and it was obvious – I had to begin with the subject. I had been in a false subjectivity, and only in the snow and silence of New York, did I finally have the appropriate vision of the book. After this I wrote the book in a few months, really – it was no problem at all. The book was practically finished before I had written one line, because the vision of the book was the solution to the problem. And – finally – maybe this is why I am not against mysticism, after all, I have had my mystic experience in the snow of New York. It's another American story. And so, not only was the first book saved by American appreciation, but the second exists because of a mystic experience in New York.

I want to now give you some experience of the difference between the two books, because, after all, it is an exercise concerning what I have been speaking about – the first beginning, and the second beginning. I will read to you two lectures: the first is from just after *Being and Event* – not just after but from 1994 – and the second is from just after *Logics of the Worlds* – it is from 2007. So I will read the first, and after that I will give you the text. And tomorrow, I shall read you the second lecture. Ultimately, all of this is just so you have a perception, an idea, of the difference, and so a perception of the two styles of philosophy. I will read the first lecture of 1994, the title is: *The Ethic of Truths: Construction and Potency*. I will not read the beginning to you – you will have the text.

> "Modern philosophy is a criticism of truth as
> adequation. Truth is not *adequation rei et*

intellectus. Truth is not limited to the form of judgment. Hegel shows that truth is a path. Heidegger suggests that it is a historic destiny.

I will start from the following idea: a truth is, first of all, something new. What transmits, what repeats, we shall call *knowledge.* Distinguishing truth from knowledge is essential. It is a distinction which is already made in the work of Kant: the distinction between *reason* and *understanding.* It is a capital distinction for Heidegger: the distinction between truth, *aletheia,* and cognition or science, *techne.*

If all truth is something new, what is the essential philosophical problem pertaining to truth? It is the problem of its appearance and its "becoming". A truth must be submitted to thought, not as a judgement, but as a process in the real.

[...]

For the process of a truth to begin, something must happen. What there already is, the situation of knowledge as such, only gives us repetition. For a truth to affirm its newness, there must be a *supplement.*"

Just as a commentary: in *Being and Event* the event is conceived not only as a cut in the situation but as a supplement of the situation – it is something which is near Derrida, by some aspects – and so for a truth to appear in its newness there must be a supplement.

"This supplement is committed to chance. It is unpredictable, uncalculable. It is beyond what is. I call it an event.

A truth appears, in its newness, because an eventful supplement interrupts repetition.

Examples: the appearance, with Aeschylus, of theatrical tragedy; the irruption, with Galileo, of mathematical physics; an amorous encounter which changes a whole life; or the French Revolution of 1792.

An event is linked to the notion of the *undecidable*. Take the utterance: "This event belongs to the situation". If you can, using the rules of established knowledge, decide that this utterance is true or false, the event would not be an event. It would be calculable within the situation. Nothing permits us to say: here begins a truth. A *wager* will have to be made. This is why a truth begins with an *axiom of truth*. It begins with a decision. The decision to *say* that the event has taken place.

The fact that the event is undecidable imposes the constraint that a *subject* of the event must appear. Such a subject is constituted by an utterance in the form of a wager. This utterance is as follows: "This has taken place, which I can neither calculate, nor demonstrate, but to which I shall be faithful"."

So the question of the event – in *Being and Event* – is directly in correlation with the subject. The event exists, naturally, but we have no proof, and no demonstration of that sort of existence. The only attestation, the only proof of the event, is the decision of the subject, the decision of this new subject. The decision of the subject says: 'This has taken place, the event is real, I can neither calculate, nor demonstrate this point, but I shall be faithful to my decision'.

> "A subject is, to begin with, what fixes an undecidable event, because he takes the chance of deciding it.
>
> This engages the infinite procedure of the verification of the true."

So you see: the beginning of a truth is a decision and the process of the truth is the verification of this decision. We cannot have any guarantee at the beginning – the guarantee is retroactive. The guarantee is the retroactive verification that my decision was a true decision, and so it is in the consequences of the decision and not in the decision itself, and that is why we have this infinite procedure of the verification of the true.

> "It's the examination, within the situation, of the consequences of the axiom which decided the event. It's the exercise of fidelity. Nothing regulates its course, since the axiom which supports it has arbitrated outside any rule of established knowledge."

All this is outside of any rule, any fixed rule, of the situation itself. We have no knowledge which could be the orientation of the process. We have it only in the consequences of the first and pure decision.

> "It is then a hazardous course, or a course without a concept."

So the process of a truth is a process without concept.

> "But what is a pure choice, a choice without a concept? It's obviously a choice confronted by two *indiscernible* terms. Two terms are indiscernible if no effect of language permits their distinction. But if no formula of language distinguishes two terms of the situation, it is certain that the choice of having the verification pass by one rather than the other can find no support in the objectivity of their difference. It is then an absolutely pure choice, free from any presupposition other than that of having to choose, with no indication marking the proposed terms; the choice by which the verification of the consequences of the axiom will first pass."

All that is very important. The event happens, but in some sense it is only the subject who confirms that the event happened, and so it's a decision. After the decision we have a process of verification – term by term – of the decision, but there is no objective, that is, no existing knowledge of the situation, which can orient the choice, because if you were to have some such knowledge then the event would not be an event, but something that is a part of the situation. And so we are confronted after an event with a succession of pure choices – pure choices that are not irrational, but are not included in the knowledge inside the situation, and so are not inside the world. There is, then, something that must be decided on without any guarantee for that sort of decision, and such a succession of choices is the process of a truth – a process without any guarantee in the given, existent knowledge of the situation.

> "This means that the subject of a truth demands
> the indiscernible. The indiscernible organizes the
> pure point of the subject in the process of
> verification. A subject is what disappears between
> two indiscernibles."

This is a definition of the subject: a subject makes pure choices, and so it is a series of choices between indiscernible terms. And, in fact, the subject is something like a disparition between these choices of one term over another. Finally, we can say that a subject disappears between two indiscernibles.

> "A subject is the throw of the dice which does not
> abolish chance, but accomplishes it as a
> verification of the axiom which founds it. What
> was decided concerning the undecidable event
> must pass by *this* term, indiscernible from its
> other."

So we must decide, but we must decide between two indiscernible terms, and we decide in the form of our conviction that the consequences of the indiscernible event must pass by this term.

> "Such is the local act of a truth. It consists in a
> pure choice between two indiscernibles. It is then
> absolutely finite.
>
> For example, the world of Sophocles is a subject
> for the artistic truth that Greek tragedy is, a truth
> initiated by the event of Aeschylus. This work is
> creation: pure choice in what, before it, was
> indiscernible. And it is a finite work. However,
> tragedy itself, as artistic truth, continues unto
> infinity. The work of Sophocles is a finite subject

of this infinite truth.

In the same way, the scientific truth decided by
Galileo is pursued unto infinity. But the laws of
physics which have been successively invented are
finite subjects of this truth.

We continue with the process of a truth. It began
with an undecidable event. It finds its act in a
finite subject confronted by the indiscernible. The
course of verification continues; it invests the
situation with successive choices."

That is the point, and we can experiment all of that. For
example, in the course of a love, a true love, we have successive
choices. The construction of a truth is always in the form of
successive choices, and there is no determination in the
succession of choices. If you have a determination by
knowledge, then there is no construction of something new. I
return to the beginning of the text: a truth is fundamentally
something new, something not reducible to the pure context of
the situation. And why is such a construction the construction of
something new? Precisely because it is not determined by the
situation – if it was determined by the situation it would not be
something new. And so we must include in the definition of
truth that truth is constructed by a succession of choices that are
not simply the execution of determination inside the situation.
This – finally – is why the progressive construction of a truth is
something in relationship with pure chance: the chance of the
event and the successive chances of pure choices, without any
complete determination. And I think you can refer to your
experiences of participation in a truth in your life – in political
engagement, in an acceptation of a great love, in the effect of a
work of art, and so on – to understand this point.

In any case we have to make choices precisely there where they are not determined by the terms of the choice, and so there is something like a pure or instinctive choice which is in the dependency of an event and which is a choice to be faithful to the event by the choices themselves. And maybe it is a correct choice, and maybe it is not – that is the point. We cannot have a primitive certainty concerning the correctness of such choices, *but we must make them*. It is these types of choices and their deployment within the situation which constitute the construction of a truth.

> "Little by little the contour of a subset of the situation is outlined, in which the eventful axiom verifies its effects. It is clear that this subset is infinite, that it remains interminable. Yet it can be stated that if we suppose it to be ended, it will ineluctably be a subset that no predicate unifies. An untotalizable subset."

This is the most difficult point. The idea is that by successive choices we construct something new *in the situation*, the name of which is truth. *We are in the situation*, and so this construction is not something in the sky – the construction of a truth is a terrestrial process, a human process. We are in a situation, *always*, and we construct – by successive choices – something new. And this something new is – from an ontological point of view – purely and simply a subset of the situation, it is a singular collection of elements of the situation. Again, because we are inside and not outside of the situation, a truth cannot but be a subset of the situation. But this subset cannot be made by the world as it is, by the situation as it is, simply because if this was the case this subset would not be something new. If, for example, the subset is a subset of cars within the situation, or a subset of tables, and so on, naturally it is not something new. If we have a name within the situation to designate the new subset, then the subset is not new, because it would be a subset that is recognizable in the situation and before the event, by some existing name. *A subset is new only if it is without name, that is, only if it is unrecognizable in the situation from the point of view of knowledge.*

It is not easy either to understand how, or even to accept that, there can be a constructed subset in the situation that cannot be recognizable by the knowledge of the situation. But if it is a subset constructed by pure-choices, then there is no determination of it, and so there cannot be any recognition by the knowledge of the situation. And so, such a subset cannot have a name, it must be – as we have said – anonymous. There is, then, a relationship between a succession of free choices constitutive of a subset of a situation – but without any reference in the situation – and the construction of a truth. And, finally, this is why a truth cannot be part of knowledge – and the two, in fact, are distinct.

Maybe, the simplest example of all of this is the case of love. The event is a pure encounter between somebody and somebody else, and the decision that it is an event is a declaration, for example, the declaration 'I love you'. And what is the signification of something like that? It is exactly the decision that such an encounter with somebody is an event and not something within the law of the situation – it is something absolutely new in your life, and the translation of that is always a declaration. And a declaration cannot be but a decision. We are, of course, in the hypothesis that it is a true decision and not a false decision, that is, that you are not saying 'I love you' for sexual reasons and so on. But after that we must construct something which is the real of that love, and we perfectly know by our experience that for that we have to make some free choices, a succession of free choices – concerning sexuality, organization, a child, and so on. All of that must be decided, and, naturally, there is nothing in the situation – no knowledge, no law – which authorizes that sort of choice, which determines it for you. Ultimately, you must invent the law of the choice, because the law of that choice does not exist – it does not pre-exist the choice – and so every love is singular, every love is a creation. Finally – through this succession of choices – you construct a subset of the situation, which is the real of your love, and it is a subset without any name in the situation. Certainly you can have an abstract name – it is 'a love' – but the name of this concrete love does not exist, naturally. Maybe you also invent a name – our love is named....

All of that, finally, is a truth – it is the process of a truth. A truth is a construction: a truth is under this paradigm of an event, a decision concerning this event, a succession of free choices, the construction of a subset, and this subset is a subset without name, a subset which is not included within the knowledge of the situation, finally, a truth is not only not named in the situation and not in its knowledge, but it *cannot be in the knowledge*, because it is the result of successive free choices without any existent law in the situation itself. And this sort of subset is a generic subset. And it is, maybe, the central concept of *Being and Event*: a generic set is a set which is not included in the knowledge of the situation, and, in this sense, it is really a new subset, a new subset within the situation, and a subset which is without name, without place in knowledge, and which is something like a supplement to the situation. And that, finally, is the solution to the problem of what is the being of a truth – the being of a truth is a generic set. So *Being and Event* was a response to a problem, and this is the solution of this problem.

So we stop here. I have read only a part of the text, but I give the text to my savior... who is without name... okay, my savior is here. You take the text and you give a copy to everybody.

4.2 Discussion I

We can begin. Lionel is here because, like Wallace Stevens, he speaks both languages completely. And so in case of an oral discussion – which is a possibility – Lionel can explain to me the point if it is obscure for reasons of hearing or understanding. So, today we will discuss not the questions of today – which we will, instead, discuss tomorrow – but the questions of yesterday. I propose a classification of the questions: some questions on the anthropological nature of philosophy, then some concerning the dialectical nature of philosophy, and dialectics more generally, and finally specific questions concerning the concept of immanent exception.

Lionel will read the questions. The first question on the anthropological nature of philosophy is a question of Cecilia. And, what is the question?

Question 1: If indigenous societies are incapable of philosophical investigation within their own traditions and in their own languages, how can they participate as individuals and as societies in the production of a future, without abandoning their cultures and becoming westernized? Is philosophy necessary or desirable in such a case? Is it possible that western philosophy lags behind indigenous traditions regarding the interrelatedness of living beings and natural phenomena?

[Badiou]: Thank you for this question – which is, in some sense, a central question today: it is the question of the relationship between dominant societies and poor societies, or weak societies, in the contemporary world. I want to explain that the question of universality is not first a question of philosophy. The question of universality is – in my language – the question of the existence of truths. But, finally, the question is of the existence and the creation of something that is of universal value. That sort of creation is not primitively in the field of philosophy – it is an artistic creation, a scientific creation, a political creation, a human creation in general, they are creations concerning the signification of life, and so on. And we must affirm that the possibility of that sort of creation exists in all societies. And so we are not at all saying that the possibility of universal truth is a possibility exclusively inside the western world, not at all. Philosophy is something particular, and, in some sense, not universal across the western world itself. Philosophy is what is possible after something else, it is a thought, a form of thought, that is possible only in a second moment, because the condition for the existence of philosophy is the existence of some truths – artistic creations, for example, or mathematical inventions, great loves, some great poems, and so on. All of this must exist *before* philosophy, *and independently of philosophy*. It is the case that in some circumstances philosophy does not exist, but there are also cases where philosophy exists. *Philosophy comes after*, after the real processes of truths. And I have given some examples of truths which certainly are the creations of societies which are not inside the western world, like African sculpture, various visions of our relationship to nature, and so on, and so on. And so, for philosophy it is a question, *a duty, an obligation*, of taking into account *all creations the value of which is or can be universal*, and not at all only creations from the western world. Philosophy must think all creations that can be understood universally, all creations that can come back to life, if you want, in any country, in another world. That is the first point.

The second point is that while philosophy was a local creation it was *and it is* addressed to everybody. And so, where philosophy does not exist the task of the philosopher is first to understand that in that sort of society without philosophy truths exist – original creation exists – and to take account of this in the field of philosophy, and secondly, to explain why philosophy does not exist in all cultural contexts. But, after that, philosophy must also account for why – by way of contact with new truths – philosophy is possible in that particular determinate culture.

And so, there is no contradiction between the local existence of philosophy and the existence of societies and cultures that are not historically enclosed in the western world. There would be a contradiction only if philosophy was the affirmation that truths exist or that they can be created only in the western world – and this would be, in fact, an imperialist position. But, on the contrary, we must affirm –especially today, and philosophy is no exception here – that the existence of truths, of the existence of creativity concerning universal truths, is not at all limited to the western world, but – and as the evidence suggests – that there exist many things outside the western world, which are of universal value. And, finally, the task of philosophy – in particular of the political part of philosophy – is to fight against the idea that the western world is a good world. It is not at all the case that because philosophy is a creation of the western world that it must confirm that it is a good world. In fact, by the creation of philosophy the western world created something that is largely the place of the critique of the western world itself. And it is – across the history of philosophy – the great tradition of philosophy to be the strong critic of its proper world, that is, to fight against the monopolization of the human destiny by the western world.

And so the question was absolutely a good question. And, finally, it points to why it is so important – in my conviction – to say that philosophy is under conditions. *There is no pure autonomy of philosophy, it is under conditions, it is under the condition of the existence of truths.* And so, if the existence of truths is not by necessity inside this world but exists in all forms of worlds, then the consequence is that philosophy is under the condition of the existence of the multiplicity of cultures, and not one culture.

There is now an anonymous question.

Question 2: You spoke yesterday about the effect of demonstrative mathematics in philosophy, in Greece. Do you believe that quantum physics has had, or will have, an effect on contemporary philosophy? Has it influenced your thinking in any way?

[Badiou]: This is an example of the question of the conditions of philosophy. And I absolutely affirm that developments in science, or by science, are always important conditions for the development of philosophy.

You perfectly know, for example, that the beginning of philosophy would be impossible without the birth of mathematics, more specifically, of demonstrative mathematics in Greece. And so, it is a good question to ask whether this sort of revolution in the field of physics – like the creation of quantum mechanics, for example – has effects in the field of philosophy. And my response, naturally, is yes. And, certainly, the most important consequence of this development is that by the mediation of quantum mechanics we have the eruption of probability into the vision of the natural world, we have – as a result of quantum mechanics – a not-completely deterministic vision of physics.

During the first part of the last century there were two revolutions in the field of physics: first, relativity, and second, quantum mechanics. The problem, as you know, is that these two revolutions are not exactly in accord, the problem is that there is a great tension between them. But, certainly, relativity has changed the philosophical conception of time. After the purely linear conception of time in Newtonian physics, we have a new conception of time, which is in close relationship to space. And space and time, as you all know, are, in some sense, the true framework for the description of nature. And so we are in a universe with four dimensions, and not only three. In the same direction, quantum mechanics has informed philosophy of the relation of determination and chance, or determination and contingency. And this inclusion of contingency, of chance, in fact, shows a sense in which my conception is opposed to that of classical metaphysics, where truth is always in a close relationship with determination, with necessity. The only exception to this relationship was – *sometimes* – the grace of God. But in the field of sciences proper, truth was always associated with a deterministic vision of nature. With quantum mechanics we have something different.

We could say that my inclusion of the event into the definition of truth has a certain correspondence with the idea of indetermination in quantum mechanics. In fact my master Althusser – many years ago – also proposed a materialism that included some effect of chance, he called it aleatory materialism. And so, once again, my answer to the question is yes – yes the existence of quantum mechanics has had an effect on philosophy.

I think that today it is impossible to say, to maintain, that the fundamental and unique relation in nature is the relation between cause and effect. If you read Spinoza or Descartes, for example, for them it is evident that all relationships in nature are of the form of the relationship of cause and effect, and their vision, naturally, was a deterministic vision of nature as a system of necessities. I think that under the condition of modern science it is impossible to maintain this point of view, precisely because we must understand that in nature itself – not only human nature, but nature itself – there is a part of un-determination.

These two questions were questions concerning the context of philosophy, the anthropological nature of philosophy. And now we have a question concerning the dialectical nature of philosophy – it is a technical question, but a historical and philosophical question too. It is a question from Jake.

Question 3: Hegel distinguishes the particular from the singular as the description of the object, or subject, and the object, or subject in itself. The singular in its uniqueness has a universal quality. Does your relation between the particular and universal ignore this third term – singularity? If so, why?

[Badiou]: Naturally, if we have to think something that is, in some sense, in a particular context, and, in another sense, universal, certainly we must say like Hegel that there is a singularity of that sort of thing, that that sort of thing is singular. Singularity, in Hegel, is something like a synthesis of particularity and universality. And we must assume this point: a truth is a singularity, absolutely. And it is very important to say that a truth is not a generality but a singularity. For example, a truth is a sequence of works of art, a scientific theory, a specific love, and so on. A truth exists as a singularity, and there is a uniqueness to each truth – a truth is singular, always. And so it is completely opposed to the vision of truth as a judgment.

When we think of truth as the truth of a judgment, universality is the universality of the proposition. But what is the universality of a proposition? It is always to say that for every x this property is true. And so there is always something like a universal quantifier, and so it is always in the form of a generality. We again find a contradiction between our vision and the analytic point of view, in that the dialectical vision affirms that truth cannot be reduced to the generality of a proposition or judgment. A truth is a creation, a production, and there is always a unicity to a truth, a truth is always singular, it is always a singularity, in its existence.

Naturally, there are different forms: it can be the singularity of a collective action, a revolutionary collective action, and so the singularity of a political event, or it can be the singularity of a sequence of works of art, and so on. And so there are different forms of singularity, but I can say – and the question is a very good question – that, naturally, a truth is a singularity, since there is no possibility of thinking something that is particular and universal without that thing being singular, precisely because it is not the generality of a judgment but the absolute singularity of the existence of something. And this, in fact, is why the possibility of resurrection exists for that sort of thing: it can come back to life in another world, precisely because it is not an abstract generality but a concrete existence of a singularity.

[Student]: Is singularity the marriage of the universal and the particular?

[Badiou]: From a strictly logical point of view – and this is the case in Hegel, in some sense – we can define the singularity as the synthesis of universality and particularity. But, naturally, this synthesis is a little more complex – it is more complex precisely because singularity is always a process of creation and not a just a mechanical synthesis, a mechanical conjunction. To use your metaphor: the synthesis of universality and particularity is much more a birth – it is a construction of something universal *out of particularity, by particular material.* And so – logically speaking – yes: something singular is in the form of a result of particularity and universality, but it is not so abstract, because that sort of thing is not directly inside the particular. A properly universal singularity is something created out of particularity but which attains a universal value, and so it is not an abstract synthesis of the particular and the universal, since, in fact, the universal does not exist before the creation of the singularity.

If you were to say that the universal existed before, then you would have to admit that there is another world where that universal exists already, and where it has always existed. But it does not: universality is the disposition of the singularity – with its uniqueness, its origin, and its creation. We can give many examples – it is not at all very difficult. For example, a new invention in the field of artistic creation is certainly at the very beginning purely particular, it is from within a concrete situation of painting, of music, and so on, and so you create something in a field which is particular, with some historical state and so on, but the result may be singular. And so universal value is a possibility, and not a mechanical result, it is a possibility for a creation that originates in particularity. After all, it is possible – and in fact most creations are of this sort – that a creation remains in particularity and nothing more. We cannot say that such a creation is always universal, certainly. And so, a creation is first *by necessity* something made of particular means, inside a particular world, and so on, *and after that it is possible that its destiny is universality* – a destiny that has to be verified, verified by resurrection.

[Student]: If the verification of an event is constructed out of a sequence of free choices, how can this be distinguished from personal biography?

[Badiou]: There is no general law concerning this point. For example, if we have something like a political event it is localized, always – it is the revolt of students or workers *in some particular country*, at some particular time, like May '68, for example. And the individual position concerning this event is in the form of a declaration: if you engage your personal existence in the fight, in the revolt, in the movement, *it's a decision... it's a decision.* That it is a decision is clear because we know that some people make this decision and others do not. The verification of this decision is possible only through the successive consequences of that sort of decision. And there is always a mixture between something that is, in some sense, purely collective – the existence of the revolt, for instance, the objective of the revolt, and so on – and something purely individual – the decision. And so we have something like a conjunction between something collective, a collective event – which is political precisely because it is collective – and what I can name the atomic choices of individuals. But the collective is ultimately composed of individual choices, but without complete determination between the two. It is not because an event is collective that individuals are determined to be inside the event. And this is, in fact, why the consequences of an event in a situation cannot be as a pure collective necessity. Certainly there is something like that – something like a collective necessity – but it is, finally, also composed of what you call biographical decisions. And why? Why is some individual completely engaged in a situation and another is not? There is, naturally, some determination – he is a student, he is in some university where the revolt is strong, he is a worker, he has leftist parents, and so on and so on – but there is always a point where we cannot inscribe the incorporation purely by determination. Why? Precisely because – empirically speaking – we can always find someone who has the same determinations but who is not in the revolt. Determination plays a big part, certainly, but there is always a point, maybe a very small point, which is not reducible to the determination. And this part, *this small part*, is, after all, what can be named freedom. There is something of freedom in the atomic decisions constitutive of the consequences of an event.

And so we can examine a collective event from two completely different perspectives, from two different points of view: from the massive determinations, which is also correct – in the situation there are important places, important conjunctions, like the conjunction of workers and students, there are important contradictions, and so on – but we must also describe all that from the point of view of the atomic decisions of somebody, and this is, finally, inside all of this. And it is, finally, always something like the crossing of the two that constitutes the possibility of a new truth. And, in *Logics of Worlds*, I name this incorporation, the process of the incorporation of individuals into the body of a truth. But incorporation is only a possibility, it is a necessity for the process of a truth, but it is only a possibility, a possibility, naturally, open to everyone. All that there is, after an event, after some interruption, is, in fact, just a new possibility. Naturally, if there is no revolt at all the possibility of being inscribed in the revolt does not exist, but, in reverse, it is not because there is a collective event, a revolt – which is localized somewhere – that there is complete determination to be inside the collective revolt. And so, maybe it is like quantum mechanics after all: there is a collective result which at the macroscopic level is like determination, but if you focus on what is inside, on the atomic decisions, you find something which is not determined.

[Student]: What is the distinction between a decision and a judgment?

[Badiou]: A decision can be without judgment: a decision is when you personally decide to be engaged in a process, and it is not reducible to a judgment. Naturally, if you are or become engaged in some truth-process you are saying that it is a good process, and you have your reasons and so on, but all that, in the end, is a justification. But the act of decision itself *is an act, it is an act and not a judgment.* A judgment can be a justification of an act, and it can be among the reasons for the act, but, finally, to decide something is to do something and not only to say that something is good. And, in fact, in a political situation, or an existential situation in general, we can make a clear distinction between a positive judgment concerning a process and an affective participation in the process – they are not at all the same thing. This is why there is always the possibility of making a judgment but to not be inside of a movement. And this, in fact, is where I oppose Hannah Ardent, for example – for her the political is the place of judgment, but I think that this is not completely the case. We have, for example, the question not only of the political judgment but also of political action, and we know perfectly – even through experience – that it is not the same thing. There is, for one, no pure determination from a judgment to an action, and the central part of political activity is action, collective action, absolutely. And we can see this perfectly in concrete politics today: we can have a judgment concerning the government, or concerning some decision of the government, but without any change in the situation, precisely because a change of the situation is an active change not a pure question of opinion. In my country, for example, we know that the opinion, the majority of opinion, is against the government of Sarkozy, but Sarkozy continues to do the job. There is something in pure opinion which is an impotency – it is without organization, without mobilization, without action, and so on. And this, finally, is proof that the political field is not reducible to the question of opinions, but to the question of the existence of a real process, to the construction of a new political truth.

Next there is a question from Laura.

Question 4: If knowledge can be dialectical, then how and where, can it, or does it, rupture?

[Badiou]: The dialectical vision of knowledge is a vision of knowledge that includes the existence of ruptures inside the development of knowledge itself. It is only in the analytical vision of knowledge that we assume the continuity of the development of knowledge. In the dialectical vision of knowledge we have an affirmation of the existence of ruptures. And, in fact, we can see that in the history of the sciences. In the history of sciences we have definite ruptures at some points. It is not only in the political process or the artistic process, but in the scientific process too that we have very important ruptures. For example, in the passage of the conception of time in Newtonian physics to the conception of time in the physics of Einstein there is a real revolution. It is not a revolution outside of knowledge, but a revolution inside the development of knowledge itself, it is a revolution in physics. The dialectical vision recognizes that there exist ruptures in the development of knowledge, and so, knowledge is not a pure accumulation, or a pure continuity. There is really a discontinuity, an objective discontinuity in the development of knowledge, and so there is an immanent negation because, in some sense, the physics of Einstein is the negation of Newtonian physics, but in another sense it is a development and continuation of physics itself – there is a level where Newtonian physics is true, and there is another level, a more cosmic level if you want, where only relativity is true. And so it is really dialectical in the sense that in the passage from Newtonian physics to Einsteinian physics there is a synthesis of negation and construction. There is negativity inside of scientific development, absolutely. And this, finally, is why we cannot stay in the purely analytical vision of science.

[Student]: The dialectical movement of knowledge also has a practical side. How is the relationship that physics has to

knowledge different from other dialectical knowledges – in so far as in physics you can observe but not interrupt the object you are observing, that is, you can be just testing a hypothesis?

[Lionel]: So you are saying is there a difference between...

[Student]: Between dialectical knowledge in physics and dialectical knowledge in social fields?

[Badiou]: I think that there is a difference because the two determinations are not the same, and also because social contradictions have a dimension which is subjective. And so we have to take into account the negativity of consciousness, and the negativity of practical action and so on. The forms of negativity are probably not the same. Maybe in social contradictions there is something destructive – there is some conflict between enemies, there is class struggle, there are wars – and so there is a place for violence and destruction. In the development of science there is negation, there is revolution, there is brutal transformation, but it is not properly violence and destruction, because it is not in concrete reference to the notion of subjectivity, and subjectivity is there also in relation to others, and maybe, sometimes, to enemies. And so we can have a form of contradiction named antagonistic contradiction. Maybe, finally, the difference between dialectics in the social question and dialectics in the scientific question is the fact that in the social question contradiction can be an antagonistic contradiction, and so a contradiction without synthesis.

Question 5: Ruptures have been referred to as violent ruptures. Are there non-violent ruptures? What is the definition of violence? And what is the difference between 'rupture' and 'interruption'?

[Badiou]: We are, in some sense, in the same field as the last question. Violent ruptures was a metaphor, it was not the idea of violence in the precise sense of violence concerning bodies, concerning life and death and so on. When I said that ruptures are violent it was only in the sense that a rupture is really a rupture – it's a metaphor. It was to say that a rupture is a surprising transformation, something that is not in a peaceful continuation. In this sense the passage from Newtonian physics to Einsteinian physics is a violent passage and, in fact, there exist resistances, oppositions, conflicts, and so on – it was not a peaceful passage with a global consensus concerning the passage. This was the signification, the metaphorical signification of violence.

If we take violence in the sense of antagonistic contradiction – with the possibility of destruction, war, death, and so on – then my answer is that there exist non-violent ruptures. If violence is not the metaphorical designation of true change, with opposition, resistance, and so on, but something where there is a will to destroy somebody or something, to destroy completely, and to be victorious, and so on, then the rupture between the two forms of physics is non-violent. And so, for the first question my answer is connected immediately to the second question – the definition of violence – since the second is the key to the first. Violence is not a simple notion, because violence has a weak signification and a strong signification. The weak signification of violence is precisely that something happens which is like a choice, which is surprising, which is not in the quiet continuity of life, of existence, and so on, something happens, but in the radical sense, something happens which is not reducible to the state of affairs. And in this weak sense – this metaphorical sense – we can say that some experience was a violent experience – and it does not mean there was death, war, bodies suffering, and so on. Rather, all we are saying in such a case is that there is some experience of newness. In this sense an amorous encounter, for example, can be violent – as can the effect of a very impressive work of art, or the effect of a very extraordinary

film, book, and so on. In this case we define violence as a big
disruption to existence. But in its strong sense violence is really
in relationship to antagonistic contradiction, that is, to a situation
where it is impossible to find a way without the destruction of
one of the two terms of the contradiction. For example, if you
are on a real battlefield, then defeat or victory is a radical
question and we must destroy the forces of the enemy. And
violence, true violence, is under something like a law of death, it
is a question of death, in fact. And this is why we generally
name something where the question of death is present, or where
the question of suffering is present, violent. And so violence – in
the strong sense - in our world is very often the question of the
bodies of human beings, it is a corporeal question, it is a
question of torture, death, suffering, and also moral suffering.
For example, an amorous rupture – which can be a traumatic
rupture – can be very violent, and, as you know, there are
amorous murders, they exist, but it is not violent in the strong
sense of the word. Love has many truths, certainly, and it is also
dangerous, and because of this it is something violent. If we take
the weak sense, then we can say that there is violence in every
truth: a new truth, or even a resurrected truth, always has a
violent beginning, a violent newness, it is surprising, it is
something that is not really in the situation, and it is something
of universal value, something that is beyond the world as it is,
beyond the situation, and so it's a violence against that situation,
certainly, because if it becomes a truth it's proper world cannot
remain the same. But, strictly speaking – I return to the point –
violence in the strong sense is in play only in antagonistic
contradiction between two persons, to classes, and so on.

And now, the difference between rupture and interruption....
Concerning violence the question is, probably: what is the rule
concerning violence, that is, is there a moral rule over violence
in the context of a truth? And, naturally, this is also the question
of non-violence. This is an important question today, absolutely.

For example: is there a possibility of revolutionary politics today, in the context of non-violence? It is a very difficult question because what is to be done in a situation where you are non-violent but the enemy is violent? It is always a problem. And I think – I cannot develop this point because it is a very complex one, but I think – that we cannot completely eliminate the possibility of defensive violence. Aggressive violence is generally a bad thing, but the contemporary complete suppression of even defensive violence is for me a real difficulty. Precisely because you can have a situation where the very essence of the enemy is to be violent – the most famous example is fascism: fascism assumed absolutely that violence is right, and the will to destroy all of its enemies is a characteristic of that sort of politics. Suppose that you construct something which is popular, peaceful, and so on, and then you have a fascism with the will to destroy all of that, to kill everybody, and so on – here, concretely, non-violence is very difficult! And so the dialectic between non-violence and violence is a complex dialectic, concretely. And I think that today we don't completely have the measure of the problem, *and it is a problem*. You know the experience of non-violence in India, for example, but at the end of that there was extraordinary violence between Muslims and Hindus. The question is really an open question.

[Student]: To continue with this discussion on rupture. It seems that this idea of rupture as in May '68 is no longer possible, because in our advanced capitalist society all chances for rupture are automatically absorbed or mediated, and so the chance for rupture is removed. And I am thinking of September 11th in the United States, the Banlieue Riots of 2005, the anti-war protests or even the Tarmac 9. All that was absorbed or mediated and the chance for rupture never occurred. May '68 – all of the thought that led to it, the actions, the people coming together – never has the chance to occur in our society now.

[Badiou]: I understand the question... but, finally, you know, when I was in France in 1967 the situation was completely quiet, the system was excellent, there was no revolt at all, de Gaulle was celebrated by everybody. And so the interruption, the rupture of May '68, was certainly impossible. And an event, a true event, is always the apparition of something that is impossible... that *was impossible* – this is a characteristic of an event. If something is the creation of a possibility inside the situation, then it is not an event, then it is only a possibility of the situation, a rational possibility. And there are, certainly, some politicians who are saying that this position is possible: they say precisely that we can have a rational possibility inside the situation which would be a true change. But an event is precisely the making possible of something that was impossible, it is precisely the possibilization of an impossibility – that is, in fact, a possible definition of an event. And it's true, in 1966, 1967 France was a quiet country. There was intellectual activity, very dense intellectual activity, okay, but on the side of the large masses of students, workers, and so on, it was a stable situation. And nobody was speaking of revolution, abstractly yes... but as a fact it was absolutely not a possibility. And so we return – with your question – to the definition of the real by Lacan: the definition of the real is the impossible, the real of the event is its impossibility *from the point of view of the situation,* from the point of view of being and existence. And so it is rupture that is at question – a rupture is always when something that everybody thinks is impossible takes place. And what is the difference between rupture and interruption? If an interruption is only the end of a part of the situation, and if that is the end of the process then there is no rupture. For example, the interruption of somebody's life is not by necessity a rupture – we all know this very well. And so if there is a rupture then there is an interruption, an interruption of repetition, but the reverse is not the case – some interruptions are not ruptures. The question of rupture is always the question of something new, and not only of the end of something. We can return to our arithmetical image.

$$0 \mid 1, 2, 3, 4, \ldots n, n+1, \ldots \mid \omega$$

There is repetition – the creation of some differences by repetition – and there is rupture. You cannot define the rupture merely by the fact that the repetition is interrupted, for rupture there must also be something new, which is on the other side. And so a rupture, and finally an event, is not only negation – that is, the interruption of repetition – but also an affirmation, something new is here! And this is why there is a decision, the decision to say: *there is something new here.*

And there has been, and there still is, a discussion concerning May '68 on this point: many people say that '68 was not at all the beginning of something new but only the end of something – the last revolution, the last revolt, the last... and it was a discussion at that moment too. And if May '68 was a rupture then it must be the opening of a new possibility, and not only the interruption of the old possibility.

The other questions tomorrow? Okay.

5. Day Five

5.1 Lecture VIII

This morning I shall speak about the third great question concerning the relationship between philosophy and the general context of its existence: first we had the question of philosophy's anthropological determination, and second, its dialectical determination, and now, finally, we have the question of its relationship to time.

Philosophy's relationship to time has across the history of philosophy been the question of its goal, the question of the precise goal of philosophy itself. And this is a difficult question, this question of determining the precise relationship that philosophy has to time, to its time, finally. We must explain this point.

Historically we can see that sometimes philosophy is, in some sense, absolutely in its time, that it is in its moment, and that it assumes this particularity. But philosophy is also apart from its time, since it is, in some sense, the proposition to be outside of the world, outside of the contemporary world. Naturally we find these two determinations at the very beginning of philosophy, for example, in the case of Socrates. We can say that Socrates was absolutely a figure of the Greek present: he spoke to everybody in the street or the terrace, he participated in the political life of the city – he had been a director at a city council – he was also a soldier is some Athenian wars and battles, and so on and so on. He was really a citizen of his city, and he was certainly something like a public man, and not at all a secluded or retired figure. He was exposed, fully exposed to the present.

But, in another sense, he was not really inscribed in the determination of his time, in the determination of his city, and, naturally, this was interpreted by many of the citizens as a situation of absence, of contradiction, and, certainly, as something abnormal, something very abnormal. And we can see all of this in *Les Nuées*, the play of Aristophanes: Socrates is the central character in this play, but he is presented as completely abnormal, as a madman, in fact. And this representation of Socrates, of the first philosopher, is very contradictory to the idea we have of this man, who, for us, is the figure of morality, the figure of rationality, and so on. And the play of Aristophanes is a very violent play against Socrates: he is presented as something of a madman, as a purely comic character, who is not inside of the laws of the city, who is not inside of the normal practices and customs of the city, who has strange ideas, strange thoughts, strange relationships to money, to institutions, and so on and so on. And this figure of Socrates is for us strange, very strange. Between these two figures of Socrates – the Socrates in Aristophanes' play and Socrates as a man of his time, as a man inside of and participating in the city – there is a great tension, a great contradiction. And it is an example, an example of the relationship that philosophy has to its present, a relationship that is very paradoxical.

I think that this paradoxical relationship is at the very core of philosophy for abstract but fundamental reasons. The first point is that the goal of philosophy and the precisely the goal of classical philosophy is that every individual, every person, can find an orientation for his or her life. That is the goal, the concrete goal of philosophy. The theoretical goal, on the other hand, is to solve the problem of the relationship between particularity and universality, or more generally to construct a new concept of truth. We can say something like this: all philosophers construct or compose a new concept of truth, that is, a new concept of what is on the side of universality but in relationship to particularity. In fact we could say that this is a general, or minimal, definition of philosophy. But, finally, when the philosopher addresses someone, when he transmits this construction, he speaks about concrete life and not only of abstract concepts. And so there is a very concrete goal to philosophy: philosophy tries to cause a transformation of subjectivity.

There is a general idea in philosophy that in ordinary life there is no true orientation of life. That life, in fact, is a passive action, that it is determined by the laws of the situation, by one's family, by one's work, and so on, and so on. But all of these determination are, finally, at the level of necessity: they are the necessities of survival, the necessities for the continuation of life, for the continuation of a nice life, a comfortable life. Ordinary, everyday life is, finally, a life organized by the norms of the world as it is, it is life according to a correct inscription in the world as it is. But it is also a life without any consideration of the meaning of the world as it is, or of the meaning of life within that world. From this position, the world is the world because, finally, it is the world where we are, the world in which we live, and we must be inscribed in the world as it is. This is the primary injunction – we must be inscribed in the world as it is. The exception is, maybe, suicide... and it is really a philosophical question – the question of life is the question of death, certainly. But generally, we have the continuation of ordinary life, we have a complete inscription within the world as it is, and such determination *by itself* creates no real meaning for life, but only a concrete context of life. And philosophy, but also religion and some forms of wisdom and so on, – it's not an exclusively philosophical point– first explains that the world as it is cannot produce meaning for life, and so it's in part a critique of the world, a critique of ordinary life, a the critique of irreflexive life, something like that, and second, it proposes a possible meaning for life, or what I prefer to name orientation of life.

The philosophical conviction is that in its ordinary signification individual life is something disoriented, something which is a succession of decisions concerning our inscription in the world as it is, and the result is some form of organization of life, with many differences, social differences, professional differences, sexual differences and so on, but that all of that comes from outside. Life is, in fact, largely the appropriation of subjectivity to the world as it is. And so, life is a question of the relationship between inside and outside, between interiority and exteriority, between subject and the world, where the final law is on the side of the world. Why? Precisely because we must – as a sort of necessity – be inscribed in the world, we must be inscribed in the world because it is a condition of life itself. And such inscription is in a relationship to the present, and so it is, finally, a disoriented life. And why? Why is complete inscription in the world as it is a life without true orientation? Because the law of such life is also the law of the world as it is, and the world as it is has no reason to propose a true orientation of life. Finally, the law of the world as it is is the perpetuation of the world as it is.

We can, and we must, think our singularity much more, we must think our subjective interiority in such a way that our identity is – in a profound sense – indifferent to the world. Indifferent in the same way that the state, the government, the power, is indifferent to the life of the ordinary citizen. For the state we have a name, we are a number, but we are, finally, something not very important. Naturally, if we are great business men, or generals of an army, we are important, but, generally, as pure human singularities the state is completely indifferent over us. It is not our existence that is important for the state, but purely our place – we are identified with our place, in fact. If we are workers coming from some strange country, if we are immigrants, workers, poor men, and so on, from the point of view of the state we are really reduced to a number, a strict number – on pages, on papers.... And, if we have no papers we are good to be expelled. The state does not take into consideration our true interiority, we do not exist for it as subjects but only as a social places. And so, while the world is fundamentally indifferent to our existence, we cannot be indifferent to the world. There is, then, a dis-symmetric relationship between individual and world: the individual *must be inscribed in the world as it is*, but the world as it is is, finally, completely indifferent to this problem – in the case of ordinary existence, ordinary individuals, at least.

And so philosophy exists – it's *one of the many reasons for existence of philosophy*, but also of religion, and of different forms of wisdom, myth, and so on – for a very profound reason, which is to ask: what can we do to really go beyond the pure inscription of subjectivity in the world as it is? Or: what can we do to create a relationship between subjectivity and the world, which is not under the law of the world? Or, even: whether it's possible to reverse the relationship between subjectivity and the world? But for all of that we must propose a meaning for life, and not only the material means of life. And so, philosophy must propose something else than the pure material and concrete inscription of the individual inside the world as it is, it must propose some other possibility, it must open the possibility for an individual to give to his proper life real meaning, real orientation. And to not be completely determined by the outside is possible *only by a subjective movement, a subjective transformation*. But this would not be the end of determination by the outside, because if you have an orientation for life this does not mean that the laws of the world disappear. It is just the possibility to determine some orientation of life which it s *not reducible to the laws of the world as it is*. And so, finally, philosophy exists in order to create a new dialectics, a new dialectics between subjectivity and the world, or between inside and outside – it's only an image, but a correct image of this contradiction.

We can also say that the point is *to not be reduced to your place*... the point is to not be reduced to your place. And this is why philosophy always proposes another term than place for the life of individuals. But it is not only philosophy that does this, it is religion too, certainly. And this is the true sense of the religious concept of soul, because soul is precisely a definition of individuality that is not reducible to the world, to the outside. The soul is, in fact, the pure concept of the interiority, and it is a proposition with two significations. It is the religious proposition that every man or woman is identified not as a citizen, not by a place, but as a soul. And the soul is precisely the name of pure interiority, and pure interiority is not under the law of outside, but under the law of God, finally – which is maybe another form of outside, but it is not exactly the world as it is, it is something different, after all. And so we can define the signification of existence from the point of view of the soul, which is in excess to the determination by the world, by the concrete world as it is. This is the first signification of the proposition of the existence of the soul. And the second is that, in some sense, we have complete equality, because the soul of the king is not by itself better than the soul of the poor worker.

And maybe this is a fable. But you understand the very profound function of this fable? And this is, certainly, why this fable was for centuries and centuries very popular and very powerful. Why was this fable – if it is a fable... I won't answer this question... – this proposition of the existence of the soul, so very popular? Because it was the proposition of a solution, a sort of solution of the concrete contradiction between individual and society, between inside and outside, and also of the terrible contradiction between the different places of the world – between the poor and the rich, between the man with no power and the man with great power, between the slave and the free man, and so on. And so, all the terrible concrete experiences of inequality – *of radical inequality* – were in some sense reduced. As you know the position of this signification of individual life is outside the world, and so it did not reduce these inequalities on the level of concrete life, naturally, but at the level of the possible signification of individual life.

Once more, maybe it is a fable but there is a rational construction of this fable from the point of view of the question of the present: from the point of view of the question of what we can do, of what can be the meaning of life, if life is constantly terrible, unjust, and so on. If the contradiction of my individual life and the world as it is is constantly in a very oppressive form, then the proposition that the pure inside of individuality is not reducible to the law of the world is very powerful. It is powerful because it says that it is not in this world – in this world of suffering – that the meaning of existence is decided. We know, of course, that it's not a negation of suffering, there is suffering, and the suffering continues, but it is still a powerful idea. And, maybe, if there is suffering, maybe the signification of your life is by itself more positive, more positive from the point of view of the soul, from the point of view of the destiny, from the point of view of the final destiny of the individuality as such.

I say all of this – all of which you perfectly know already – because it is, maybe, the most important problem of concrete life after all. And I insist on the point that we must explain all of that – the soul, the other world, the signification of the pure interiority against the determination of the world as it is, and so on – because all that is so important, and not only in the past, not only in the past, but also today, and to millions of people. And so it is not such a strange fable after all. It is something the function of which is of capital importance in the history of humanity. What we must understand is that it's because it is really a proposition concerning the present, a proposition concerning the present life, concerning the problem of why the present life is what it is. Generally speaking, we can say that the present life is what it is because it is determined by the laws – the social laws, the political laws, the economic laws, and so on – of the world as it is. And if philosophy does not propose something for the orientation of life, we can always propose that the pure interiority is not at the level of the world as it is, but at some other level. This interiority – I repeat – is not reducible to the world as it is, to determination by outside, but the soul as irreducible to the world as it is, and our particular places in it, also depends on the idea of another world, which is the world of justice.

But what is justice? What is justice, finally? And why is the idea of justice so important in philosophy, in religion, in the politic field, but also for the state? We love to say that it is just, after all. Justice is precisely the idea of a sort of harmony between the determination by outside and the will or desire of subjectivity. Justice is the idea that it is universally possible to create a world that is not a pure contradiction between the orientation of individual life and determination by the world as it is. And we find this sort of idea in many, many forms in the intellectual and creative productions of humanity – in the religious field, in the intellectual field, in the political field, and so on.

The idea of justice is, probably, as old as humanity itself – it is not a philosophical creation, not at all. And this idea of the possibility that determination by the outside not be so completely in contradiction with subjective will, with subjective desire, is, finally, a very simple idea, but it is also – maybe – the most important idea. The idea of the soul is related to another world, but it is also in a relationship to the idea of justice because this other world – the world of the soul – is the world of justice. And so, if your soul is a good one – or maybe even if it's not, but this point is very complex... – if your interiority is in creative and good desire, then justice awaits, it awaits in this other world. In the world of justice, finally, the man of power in this world can be absolutely punished because he has been unjust.

And so the question of the present is largely the question of justice, because we can define the present from the point of view of this subjective contradiction between the idea of a proper orientation to life and the determination of life by the laws of the world as it is, by its places, and, finally, also by the demand for its continuation. Justice, then – whether in the present or in the future, in this world or another, whether by the idea of the soul or in some other way – can give meaning to the present precisely by orienting life in some other direction than the continuation of the world as it is.

The idea of the soul – as a proposition of the resolution of the injustice of the present – is also a complete subversion of the idea of the place, if place is what we are reduced to by the world as it is. It is a subversion of this idea precisely because the verdict of the world it to remain in your place, to stay in your place. And this is a very strong verdict, certainly. And it is, in fact, very difficult to not be in your place, and it is also something that very quickly becomes dangerous, very dangerous. And, generally speaking, we all stay in our place, all of us. The question of justice is, naturally, linked to that sort of determination, whether in the Marxist context, where place is defined in terms of social class, or in some different context.

And so, we can say a number of things. First, the present can be defined by the form of the relationship between external determination and interiority. This contradiction generally takes the form of the reduction of you identity to your place in the world as it is, the consequence of which is that life and existence are disoriented, that they cannot have a true meaning, because the reduction of existence to a place is also the complete absence of significance for that sort of existence. And the fact is that the world as it is is indifferent to the singularity of individuals, in general... in general. Secondly, we can say that we have a different proposition concerning this point, the name of which is justice. The proposition of justice has for a long time been principally a religious proposition, absolutely – fable or not a fable, that is another question. And there is a function to this religion determination, a very clear function, and it is why this proposition has been so popular. And we can say, finally, that philosophy too is that sort of proposition, but it is a proposition of justice not immediately reducible to the religious proposition. *But the two are not by necessity in contradiction – in fact, whether they are is a philosophical question!* In fact, more broadly, there exist many philosophical propositions that are not at all in contradiction with religious propositions, in their context. Generally, for example, classical metaphysics in the 17th century is not in contradiction – at least not in an explicit contradiction – with the religious proposition. But philosophy is, finally, another proposition.

The difference is that philosophy is, first of all, purely rational, in principle. This is the first point of difference: philosophy is purely rational, it is absolutely exposed to public discussion, its means are rational means, and there is the supposition of a logical framework common to all men and women. This is the first difference: there is no revelation, no sacred book, no fable of origins, there is nothing which is constitutive of the religious disposition in philosophy, there are only the laws of thinking, which are supposed universal. And, as a consequence – not always but very often – the proposition of justice in the philosophical framework is not the proposition of another world, but a proposition of justice that is, in some sense, *inside this world*, or by the means of a *transformation of this world, and by means which are of this world.* And so the orientation of philosophy is towards the possibility of something else inside of the world as it is, and not towards some pure existence completely outside of this world.

We can certainly define philosophy as a proposition of justice, but this definition does not create a difference between philosophy and religion, because religion too is a proposition of justice. And so if we only define philosophy as a proposition of justice, then we define philosophy as a sort of religion. Therefore, we must say something else. And this something else is precisely that philosophy is a proposition of justice, *but a proposition of justice by the means of rationality alone.* Rationality is not a precise word.... It is the proposition of just by purely human reason, by purely human means, by purely human means without any sublime power from some other world.

The absence of a fundamental fable is crucial to the definition of philosophy: in philosophy there is no elementary fable, there is no sacred book, there is no mythology, and so on. If you want: there is no story of justice, no novel of justice, but only a conceptual proposition of justice. The difference between philosophy and religion – at this point – is not over the goal, for the goal is the same. The difference is that the philosophical proposition is without any guarantee: there is no guarantee of justice by the potency of God, there is only the possibility of a purely terrestrial proposition and its realization by human means. And so, in the philosophical proposition the possibility of justice is a purely immanent possibility of the world itself. That there is this difference and this common between religion and philosophy allows us to understand why the interplay between the two has been so important across centuries.

Naturally, this possibility is not exactly a possibility of the world as it is, because the world as it is is not a world of justice. But we can open the possibility of this possibility – of the possibility of something else, finally – from within the world itself. And so there is a very important relationship between philosophy and the pure present: philosophy first proposes a new concept of justice, that is, a meaning for the present, a new way to solve the contradiction between the determination from the outside and the existence of subjectivity, and then philosophy affirms that the means of this proposition are in some way *in the present* – in the form of a possibility – and not in some other world. And this is exactly like it is in Marxism, where the proposition of justice is possible inside of the world as it is because inside of the world there is a collectivity, and the possible *organization of this fighting collectivity*, which is the means of creating the world of justice. Marxism's name for this collectivity is – as you all know – the proletariat. Marxism certainly does not say that the world as it is is the world of justice, it says, on the contrary, that it's an absolutely unjust world, but that inside of this world we can find the resources to create justice in the future. In this sense the path of Marx is of a philosophical nature, absolutely. In fact Marx thought of himself as a philosopher, a philosopher of political nature. And he is a philosopher in this sense, because the proposition of justice in Marxism is without constitutive fable and the means of its realization lie inside the world as it is, in the form of a possibility, a creative possibility. *And that, finally, is the first point*: philosophy's relation to time is a relation to the present by way of a proposition of a new orientation for the present, an orientation that is in relationship to the possibility of a new future. In this respect, philosophy is not distinct from religion, which, after all, also proposed a new future... a new future after death... or after the end of the world. And so it is a proposition of a future, but a proposition that immediately gives an orientation to the present. It is, then, what can cause immediately the possibility of life that is not disoriented, a life that is not without true significance, a life that is inscribed not only in the necessities of survival, comfort, and so on, but a life with a proper freedom.

The second point is, in some sense, opposed to the first: philosophy affirms the existence of eternal truths – again, just like religion. Eternal truths exist for philosophy in the form of universal truths, where universal means universal not only in space but also in time. And so, if a truth is really universal it can be understood not only in another world today, but also in the future, in exactly the same way that many centuries after their invention Greek mathematics can still be understood, or how we can still understand some ancient paintings, sculptures, and so on. A truth, then, is universal in both space and time, and so we can say that the universality of truth is a form of eternity. A truth is eternal precisely because although it exists in a particular world, although it is created in a particular world, in fact, it can be addressed to and resurrected in a world the time of which is unknown. Maybe it is a metaphor, but its a strong metaphor to say that a truth is eternal in this sense, that it is not reducible to any time, to any particular time, even the time of its proper origin.

Skepticism poses an objection to this eternity, because it denies that we can know truth. But, skepticism is, ultimately, a philosophy because it holds its claim that we cannot know truth to be a truth, an absolute truth, in fact – to say that we absolutely cannot know any truth, is an absolute truth. And so, we can affirm that skepticism too affirms eternal truths – it holds the truth, the absolute truth, of the impossibility of human beings knowing some truth of the world, of life, and so on. There is no exception: every philosophy – skeptic, critical, dogmatic, and so on – affirms the existence of some truth, which is posited now and forever. But this eternity is an *eternity in time, an eternity created in time.* It is a paradoxical relationship... eternity in time....

This too is something that is common to philosophy and religion: both recognize something which is not reducible to time, to it's time, something which disposes an orientation for life which is not only for today but also for tomorrow. And this, finally, is the idea of resurrection: it is the possibility that something which was dead, which was forgotten, *can return to life, can come back to life.* This is the case with the soul in religion, but it is also the case with truths in philosophy. And so, philosophy is in relation to the present by the idea of justice, and in relationship to eternity by the idea of truth.

Truth, justice, all that is very general for both... and it is what philosophy has in common with religion, because we could define religion as a proposition of a relation between truth and justice. Clearly, this is a very abstract definition, but it is also a very operative definition of religion: religion is a proposition concerning a specific relation between truth and justice. The difference is that in religion we have *the* truth, and that is not generally the case in philosophy. And *this truth* is, finally, the truth identified with God. And *this truth is the guarantee of justice – there is no religion without this conviction.*

There are, as you know, different religions, and each is, ultimately, specified by the form of the relationship between truth and justice that it proposes. The particularities of religions and their histories are very complex and sometimes obscure, but, in my conviction, each is a particular possible concrete form of the relationship between truth and justice. Certainly in each religion we have many details – you cannot eat pork, we must stop working on Sunday, you must do this, and you must not do that, and so on and so on – but, finally, what is the signification of these details? They are proofs, concrete proofs that you are in a particular religion. In themselves they are not so important, they are important in so far as observing these details is a proof of your religiosity. If you are in some religion, then you must follow its rituals, but you must follow them, ultimately, as a proof of your conviction, as a proof of your faith, in everyday life. For the philosopher such things are not so important.

And, finally, it is absolutely reasonable that those in a religion must observe it's particular rituals, because without them the conviction is too abstract, without them it is too outside of everyday life. In Islam, for example, you must pray to God five times a day, and so the presence of religion is in everyday life in the form of this obligation. But religion is not reducible to that sort of thing. And these details, which are different across religions, are, finally, very small, and depend on the specificity of particular religions, their culture, their time, their origin, and so on. Fundamentally religion is a proposition concerning the relationship between truth and justice – a truth which is a promise, a guarantee of justice. And *this* is the reason why there are so many religious people: it is not because of the details, but exactly the reverse, it is because their conviction – which gives an orientation to their lives – is in a relation to a fundamental truth, the name of which is God, and which is the promise and guarantee of justice. The rituals, the details, and so on, must be followed *because of your conviction, and because of the promise, they must be followed because they are material proofs of your religious disposition.*

The most important commonality between philosophy and religion is precisely this relationship between truth and justice, a relationship which is, finally, one between time and eternity. And in both cases this relationship is – as I have said – the existence of something eternal in time. But what is the difference? What is the difference between philosophy and religion – since philosophy is not a form of religion? The difference is that religious truth is outside of the world and not a creation of humanity, as it is in philosophy. In fact, we could say that religion and philosophy propose opposite relationships between truth and humanity: for religion humanity is the creation of truth, and so a creation of God, finally, while in philosophy is it humanity, which creates truth.

In religion, therefore, the question of justice is the question of another world, *but a world which exists.* There are two levels: the world as it is, and the other world, which is also the world of truth. Religion is the story of the existence of two levels for existence, two levels for the human destiny. The possibility of justice – the possibility of harmony between interiority and exteriority, between the will of the subject and the law of the world – is a promise of the second level, but a promise that depends on what we do on the first. Philosophy, on the other hand, is the attempt to propose the possibility of justice without the idea of two different levels of existence. Philosophy proposes the existence of truths and justice *in this world, on this level.* Truths are eternal for philosophy, but it is an eternity inside a world – truths are eternal because they can be resurrected *inside another world in the future.* And so there is a fundamental distinction between religion and philosophy, but not in the form of an explicit opposition, but in the form of the idea that philosophy is something like the attempt to realize the religious promise *here, now, and not in some other, transcendental world* – philosophy is something like the realization of the religious promise in the world of human life.

Therefore, it is not what is said in some philosophies, but that philosophy – and I insist on this point – is the will to realize religion here, that is the fundamental ground of their distinction. This is the destiny of philosophy, and it is its destiny because philosophy decided at the very beginning to be only inside the means of human thought and human practice, without any help from God and His words. There is no sacred book in philosophy, there are no fables, no mythologies, and so on, there are only arguments, definitions, propositions, and so on. This is common to all philosophies, *insofar as they are philosophies*. And if you have only human means, finally, then the proposition of justice is purely human, and if the proposition of justice is purely human, then maybe justice itself can be realized in human history. And this, finally, is why there is always something subversive to philosophy, and why it is not reducible either to the world as it is or to the religious promise. Philosophy, then, is in contradiction with the state and the church.

Philosophy is not religion and it is not the state, but it is also not scholasticism, because philosophy does not build for itself a closed institution. In the case of medieval philosophy this institution was the Church, and today it is the university – the university is the church of today, in some sense. And, in fact, the campus... the campus is very often exactly in the place of big monasteries, they are the big secular institutions of the church. Scholasticism is precisely the attempt to transform something subversive into something that is inside, that is at home in the disposition of the world as it is.

I insist on the point that philosophy and religion are important for humanity primarily because they propose the possibility of some relationship, some interdependency between truth and justice. But this relationship is not the same in both – the fact of a relationship is common, but the relationship itself is not the same. For religion the relation between justice and truth is the relation between two levels of existence: the promise is the relation between the two levels, and truth is by itself the promise of justice, and God is the name of the guarantee of that sort of promise. And so, in religion all of this circulates between the two levels. The genius of Christianity is to have a magnificent fable concerning the relation between the two levels, which is that God himself has gone from one level to the other by his

sacrifice. As a fable it is magnificent! From a theoretical point of
view its very complex – ... the father and the son,... and the
identity of the father and the son... – for instance, it's not so
simple to say that the first level has a concrete, or fetal relation
to the second. The conception in Islam, for instance, is
completely different. Finally – as I have said already – there are
many possible relations between the two levels, and we find
them in the particular religions, but what is constant across all of
them is the existence of two levels.

And philosophy too is a proposition of a relation between truth
and justice, and again – as with religion – this is why philosophy
is important. But the destiny of philosophy is to affirm the
existence of one level. That is the destiny, but it is not always
the result in concrete philosophy, philosophy is not always
successful, after all. For example, we can say that in Plato we
have two levels too: the sensible world and the intelligible
world. But if we read Plato precisely, if we read him closely, if
we try to really understand what Plato is proposing, we find that
for Plato there is only one level, finally. And, in fact, that the
distinction between the two levels is just a means for
understanding the relationship between truth and justice. In
philosophy there is really only one level, finally, which is the
level where humanity can create some truths by rational means
and by the potency of its own creativity.

In both philosophy and religion we have the idea of some
relationship of truth and justice, and that this relationship can
provide an orientation to life in the present. In the religious
vision it is because the soul is promised a second existence, and
in philosophy it is because there exists in time itself something
which is in some sense an exception to determination by time,
something which can exist in a different world. And that sort of
thing – which is precisely truth – is also a promise of justice,
because everybody is equal in front of a truth! And if the truth is

a social truth, a political truth, then everybody is equal in the world as it is. Maybe not immediately, but as a project, as a possibility.... And so, we can say that philosophy is oriented by the idea that eternity can exist in time, and that eternity is created in time, and, finally, even the very idea that humanity can create truths is, in some sense, already a form of justice. And so, for philosophy meaning in the present, meaning in our individual and collective lives, is possible by its orientation by some truth. And to orient our lives in the present by something like a fidelity to a future is precisely the point, to orient our lives by some truth is precisely the Idea.

And so the question of philosophy's relation to time is also the question of the relationship between truth and justice, and so it is also a solution of the contradiction between time and eternity. I insist on the fact that this relation is the philosophical solution of the religious promise. In philosophy there is no other level, no promise to lead us there, and no guarantee that we will enter, *but there is the existence of truths in time*. And so there is a concrete relation between the eternity of truths and the orientation of the present. This relation has had many names in philosophy – the Sartrean name is engagement, and so true life was a question of being engaged – but in all cases what is at stake is the same: we must engage our lives not only around our immediate interests, but also in the destiny of some truth.

To engage with a truth is to go beyond our place, and so we return to the first problem: to go beyond our place is the same as to support the creation of some relation between truth and justice.

Very often I accept to use religious vocabulary – and why not? They are good metaphors, after all. And so, we can say that a truth is like a grace, because it is the possibility to change your life, it is the possibility of passing from a meaningless and disoriented life to a life with an orientation, a life with real meaning. And we can also be saved, we can be saved without soul, without God, without heaven, we can save ourselves by going beyond our place... by moving collectively beyond our social determinations, by going beyond our fate. And that sort of movement is very much a redemption, after all....

And why should we not appropriate this vocabulary? Why should we not appropriate a vocabulary which has been so important and so powerful for centuries? Why not use it again in this new situation, in our situation, in a situation where we can be saved by the activity of humanity itself?

We stop.

5.2 Lecture IX

I shall stop in a half an hour, because I must do a few technical things to prepare tomorrow evening's lecture.

A concrete philosophy is always the organization of the contradiction between time and eternity. And this is, in fact, another manner by which to read philosophers: we can always ask what sort of proposition is the proposition concerning the relationship of truth and justice in a concrete philosophy. And why? Because the relationship between truth and justice is the real goal of the conceptual organization of the relationship between time and eternity, which itself is, finally, the question of truth. And so, if the most important goal of philosophy is always to propose some new meaning or some new orientation to life, this is not really different from saying that philosophy thinks the relationship between time and eternity, or even particularity and universality. But there are many possible forms of organizing this tension, this tension between inside and outside, between time and eternity, and between truth and justice. There are many possibilities, and this is why there are many philosophies.

Philosophy too is determined by the world – in some sense, at least. And so, if philosophy makes propositions against the world as it is, it makes them from within the world as it is. But if philosophers and philosophies are, in some sense, inside the world as it is, then there is a pressure, a very strong pressure, for them to assume some strict place, some strict place determined by the world as it is. And – as we have said – if philosophy assumes such a place it transforms itself into scholasticism. And such a transformation is, in fact, a form, the fundamental form, of the oppression of philosophy by the world as it is. Today, however, we have a further possible form of the oppression of philosophy: the mediatic form, which is, for example, the philosopher on television. And this new form does not transform philosophy into scholasticism, but into something like propaganda. This is very important, and there are many details of which we could speak, but what is most important for us to understand is that these forms of oppression, transformation and disfiguration of philosophy are immanent possibilities of the fact that philosophy is, *in some sense*, inside the world.

The determination of philosophy by the world can be both negative and positive. Negative determination is the prescription of a place: if you are a philosopher you must be in the university, and you must be quiet. And as you know, we can do many things in the university – it is a sort of zoo for young men and women: you can think many things, you can ask many questions, and so on – and the young beast is very dangerous.... The problem is precisely that the university has a very poor relationship to the outside. And so, while many things can be done and many things can be thought, many questions can be asked, and so on, by this young beast and by philosophy in the university, all of this remains completely within the laws of the world. And why? Precisely because the world, naturally, does not permit violent organizations against power, and so philosophy is permitted *only so long as it remains in its place, it is permitted only so long as it is without relation to what is outside of its place.* And when philosophy is strictly in this place – when philosophy accepts this place – then philosophy progressively becomes scholasticism. It's really very simple.

All of this poses a problem, a real problem, for philosophy. And why? Because philosophy is not scholasticism, and so it must resists the logic of places, and yet we also cannot completely escape the logic of places. And so philosophy must be both inside and outside, it must be inside the university but not completely.

All of this is the negative determination, the oppressive determination of philosophy by the world. But there also exists a form of positive determination of philosophy, which is its relationship to the new truths of the contemporary world. And this determination places philosophy not into a relation with the world as it is, but precisely into a relation with things that are beyond the laws of the world. In fact, it is this determination that makes philosophy contemporary.

Philosophy, therefore, is determined by the world in two distinct ways. The first determination is by its place. As you know, there is always a place for philosophy, but this place is not always the same: the place of philosophy in Ancient Greece and the place of philosophy in Medieval times, or in 17th century Germany are not the same as the place assigned to philosophy today. This determination must be resisted because philosophy, finally, does not have a place. In fact, it was Socrates who first said that philosophy has no specific place, and it is why he was everywhere, and why he spoke to everyone. And, finally, it was also because of this that he was killed – *he was killed, it's a fact.* And so there is a contradiction between the state and philosophy, between a world and something that is without place. The complete freedom of Socrates, the complete freedom of philosophical thinking is something dangerous... it is dangerous to the stability of a world, to the stability of any strict logic of places. And this is a very important story – the first philosopher was killed, we killed him because he refused a specific place, he was killed because something of philosophy opposes the logic of places. After this, philosophers had to consider the question of places as a real problem.

I know this problem personally. After all I have been in my place – I have been inside the university – but I have also been outside of this place: I have been outside of the political determination, I have been involved in political action, I have been in contact with theatre, and so on. And, in fact, my life, the orientation of my personal life, has been organized around this contradiction of place and the outside-of-the-place. And this tension is not at all simple, it is not at all easy, and it is also very complex, because sometimes the two are really in tension, sometimes there is no way of resolving that sort of dialectics. But my situation is only an example, a concrete example, of this problem of the determination of philosophy by the world.

The positive determination – I repeat – is to be in a relationship to new truths outside of philosophy, new truths in the world, and not only to be in your place. And so, as philosophers we must be in a relationship to new attempts to create something new in politics, for example. Not because we are... but because *as philosophers we must, necessarily, be in a relationship to new truths*. In fact, it is only if we are in such a relationship – and not only to politics, but also to new creations in science, in mathematics, in art, in love, and so on – that philosophy is contemporary, that philosophy is of its time.

This is the first consideration: philosophy's relationship to the present is across the dialectic of its negative and positive determination. The negative determination, which is the oppressive determination, must be resisted – we must resist the solitary place of philosophy – and the positive determination – which is the relationship philosophy must have to truths outside of itself –must be pursued. Philosophy – philosophers – must be in a relationship to new forms of creativity and new methods of engaging in the process of truth, *absolutely... absolutely*.

The next problem is the dialectic between the present and eternity. I propose to give you a few examples of the possible ways of organizing this dialectic. The first possibility is not exactly philosophical, but it is very interesting: it is the idea that we can have something like a pure present, a pure present in the strong sense, that is, we can have eternity itself in the experience of the present. You can recognize that this is the mystic position. In the mystic organization of the relation between the present and eternity it is a question of an immediate experience: in the mystical experience we have an indiscernibility between the pure present and eternity, because in mysticism the experience of the pure present is the experience of nothingness, and it is the access to the experience of the presence of God. And God, finally, is eternity in its most radical form, in its greatest form, and so His pure presence is something like the intervention of eternity in the present. But this is not a philosophical possibility because, finally, it is not a conceptual organization of thought. As you know Deleuze has defined philosophy as the creation of concepts, and here, certainly, we have creation but no concepts. And, naturally, in the mystical experience there is no creation of concepts, there is only the proposition of the possibility of an immediate relationship between these two levels, between the present and eternity. Finally, in the mystical possibility we have a fusion of the two levels – the level of the present, the level of time, and concrete life, and the level of eternity, the level of the soul, the level of God and so on – in a single point. And this point is something exceptional, it not at all a constant experience, but something mysterious, something ephemeral, something like a miracle – the mystical experience is something like a miracle in life itself, not a miracle which comes from outside, but a miracle inside of life, it is the point of the miracle inside of life itself.

Maybe philosophy can be oriented in the same direction as mysticism, but it cannot be mysticism. At most, maybe philosophy can be considered as a preparation for that sort of experience – maybe, it's a possibility. And we have something

like that in Kierkegaard, for example, and probably, also in Plato
– in Plato we find everything, because it's in a sense the
beginning, and the beginning is something where everything is
present. We find something like this in Plato because when Plato
explains the experience of the Idea, of the Idea of the Good, of
the supreme Idea, there is something which is not of a purely
conceptual nature. Plato does not completely explain what
happens here, he says something, but he does not explain it
completely – in fact very often Plato does not explain fully, he
says something but does not completely explain the
consequences. But we can understand something like that,
because complete rational knowledge, the achievement of
rational knowledge, is beyond rational knowledge, the
philosophical achievement of knowledge and so the fundamental
orientation of life goes beyond the concept. Somewhere there
Plato writes that the Idea of the Good is beyond the Idea, that it's
not reducible to the Idea, that the Ideality of the Idea is beyond
the Idea… something like that.

And this sort of vision is linked to the first possibility for
treating the dialectic of time and eternity, that is, it is a vision
not completely separate from something like mystical
experience, where we have the proposition of a point of
indiscernibility between time and eternity. In fact, when a mystic
writes a poem or prose about his experience there is no question
of time, there is no question of time because time dissipates into
eternity itself. The pure present is the presence of eternity,
certainly. And so, finally, it is not a philosophical possibility –
philosophy can be in this direction, but it cannot be mysticism.

As a commentary – a biographical commentary – I can
understand such a moment in another sense, I can understand it
in the context of an experience of an event. The experience of an
event is a historical experience, and so it is not a mystical
experience, but when you are completely absorbed in an event,

when you are of the conviction that a new world is really possible, and maybe even that the new world is here, that it is beginning, and that you are participating in the beginning of a world, there is something like a disparition of time, because it becomes a pure present. But it is not a pure present in the form of an instant cut between past and future, but a pure present in the form of a big present, a dilation of the present, a present which is not just a present. Maybe we can name that sort of experience an experience where truth and justice are the same thing, where history and orientation of life are the same thing. And there was such an opening in May '68, in fact, at the beginning – there was something like that in May '68, and it is not just my conviction. There is something like abstention in the tension of an event, in the form of an indiscernibility between past, present and future.... There is something different, something like a new time, in fact. And this new time is for everybody a time of truth, a moment where the dictatorship of outside is interrupted, a moment where the dictatorship of the world as it is is interrupted. And so there is a space of freedom opened, which is very near, very near a mystical experience, maybe it is a historical mysticism, if you want – something like that. There is a subjective tension in such a moment, and a subjective transformation, and so in such a moment something that was impossible before, something that was absolutely impossible *becomes possible*. And so in the midst of an event you are not in the constraints of time, and, in fact, there is something like an opening of time itself for the production or the invention of a new time. And so, we can say that mystical experience is the image of the experience of an event.

Certainly in a true event we have the beginning of a new time, and this new time is in some sense the time of truth. And so, it is not really an ordinary time, under the constraint and the oppression of the law of the world. It is a radical experience of freedom, if you want. Not freedom in the ordinary sense of the word – 'I can do what I want', 'I am free to say all that I want to say', and so on – it is not the freedom of any right, but *an absolute freedom, it is the freedom to create a new world.*

All of this is just to say that that sort of possibility is not solely a mystical invention, or a religious vision, but something common to experiences of some new relation between time and eternity.

I can give three other examples. Another possibility is to think that time is the realization of eternity. In this case, eternity is related to time in the form of becoming, so that time is the immanent realization of something of eternal nature. There are two versions of this conception. The Hegelian conception is that time is the realization of the Absolute. And so historical time itself is not in contradiction or in tension with eternity, but is itself its realization. And so history, the history of thought, the history of art, the history of religion, and so on, all of these, in the end, are steps in the direction of the complete realization of the Idea, the Absolute Idea. And the Absolute Idea is something like the recapitulation of all of becoming. Hegel's is another possibility to realize the conjunction of time and eternity. It is the opposite of mysticism, because mysticism is a point, a point of time where there is an indiscernibility of time and eternity, and it – on the contrary – is a conception where the totality of time is the creation of the Absolute Idea. The other possibility of time as the realization of eternity is the idea that it is not history but life, the potency of life, which is the realization of eternity. This is not Hegel, but Bergson, Nietzsche and, finally, Deleuze. It is the idea that the tension between truth and justice, between time and eternity, is resolved in the constant creative capacity of life itself. It is life which goes beyond time, life is what from within time can go beyond time. And in Deleuze we can find clear considerations concerning the immanence of eternity, and, certainly, life is the name of the immanent potency.

There is a third possibility, which is of a much more metaphysical nature, which proposes that the present is largely a delusion. In this conception the idea is that the world as it is is only an illusion with no real being, and that real being is outside of the world. And so eternity is itself the truth of the world, but to this real being we have no access, and so even our conception of it is an illusion, an illusion created by some projections from within our existence. This is a metaphysical idea that there is something like God, and that this something is not only on another level, but that it is the true real. And so, the world is pure illusion, and above this illusion we find, finally, the true real and the true real is eternal. And this is, once again, the formula of Plato, because for Plato time is an image of eternity. And if time is just an image of eternity, then the radical solution to the problem is that time does not exist, that it does not really exist. Time, then, is a sort of veil and behind the veil we have the real, but the real is not in time. And so, at the very beginning of philosophy we have the question of the relation between time and eternity, a question resolved by the idea that time is but an image of eternity. Today, naturally, we can find many versions of this conviction that the relationship between eternity and time is that eternity is the very essence of time, and that time, finally, is nothing, and so the relation between eternity and time is the relationship between being and nothingness. And this can be a purely philosophical vision because if you read Sartre – *Being and Nothingness...* being and nothingness – you see that for Sartre being as such is eternal, purely eternal. Being – being *qua* being – is for him something indifferent, something eternal, something without form, without signification, and, finally, pure being is without any time. It's something like a massive indistinctness of all that is. And time, for Sartre, is on the side of nothingness. But this nothingness is for Sartre human freedom, it is consciousness. And *consciousness is negativity, absolutely*, it is negativity and freedom, and it is this negativity, it is consciousness, which introduces something like distance, time, signification, and so on, into this closed and indiscernible mass.

And so within the conception that eternity is on the side of being and time on the side of consciousness, human existence, and so on, there are two possibilities: the Platonic version is that the real is eternity and time an illusion, but the Sartrean version of the same idea is the reverse, it is precisely that nothingness is creative, that this nothingness is the human destiny, and that being as such is pure stupidity. And you must understand that the same idea can in philosophy have two opposed meanings: for Sartre time is on the side of nothingness and eternity on the side of being, and it is the same for Plato, but for Plato – and for a great tradition, including Schopenhauer and many others – this signified that our life in time has no value and no effect, and that the truth is only on the side of eternity. But for Sartre? *The exact opposite*! For Sartre it is exactly the opposite: true life is on the side of nothingness and freedom, and on the side of being we find stupidity, reaction, political reaction and so on, because freedom is always negativity. And so, if you are a Sartrean and you are on the side of freedom, then you are on the side of nothingness, and not on the side of being.

Another possibility is that eternity is created in time – it is my position. It is the paradoxical idea –and it is, in some sense, *absolutely paradoxical* – that eternity is a form of truth, but that it is also a result, a creation, a human creation. And so, it is the idea that the eternal is created *in time*, and that it can be understood and can come back to life *in other worlds, in time*. The eternal *is created in time but can be resurrected in another time*, in another world, and so it is also somehow beyond time, beyond the time of its creation, but also beyond any particular time. And so the dialectics of this conception is not that eternity is a result of time, or time the manifestation of the eternal, as in Hegel, nor that eternity is another level of existence, like in religion, nor that the eternity is the same as time, as in mysticism, nor, finally, that time is an illusion, a veil, and that eternity is on the side of being. Rather, the idea is that eternity is the qualification of something that is created in some particular world, of something that is a generic part of the world, but also of something that is *absolutely the result of human labour, of human thought.*

To complete all of this we must examine the signification of this paradox of something eternal being created in time. We must explain this because in religion eternity is not on the side of the creation but on the side of the Creator, it is on the side of God, who as infinite and eternal creates the world as it is. But in the vision that I have proposed it is, in some sense, the reverse: it is inside of worlds as they are... *as they are,* that there exists the possibility of creating something eternal, maybe even God, for example.

Naturally, there are many objections to such a proposition – after all, if something is created, how can it be eternal? The first philosopher who said that something could be eternal *and created* was Descartes. In the theory of Descartes – in the *strange theory of Descartes* – we find the idea of the creation of eternal truths. And, in fact, creation of eternal truths is an expression of Descartes. In the case of Descartes they are creations of God, but *they are created, that is the point – there is a creation of eternal truths.* Descartes explains that something like $2 + 2 = 4$ is created, that such elementary truths – truths for whose eternity we have evidence and proof – are created. They are created because for God it was a possibility to create something different. This argument is very difficult to understand, it is very difficult to understand, but the idea is absolutely fundamental for Descartes. And, in this sense I am Cartesian: I affirm the possibility that something eternal can be created, but not by God, as with Descartes, but by a concrete human process in history.

And so we must define eternal exactly as Descartes had to define it. It is very important to understand that in Descartes it is *eternal* truths that are created. And so we have to propose a definition of truth that allows the possibility that truths – specifically truths, not anything else, but truths – can be eternal and created. For me, naturally, it is very important that a complete metaphysician like Descartes proposes such a vision. Descartes' proposition is from within a different context, certainly, but he proposes – and it is a fully rational proposition – the existence of something both created and eternal, in the form of truth, naturally. And so we have something that is eternal in existence, something that once it exists is eternal. Before? No, naturally. Before it is created it does not exist, and so is not eternal, but after... once it is created, it is eternal. Something cannot be eternal or not-eternal if the thing does not exist... *but the moment it is created, the moment that it is born, it is the birth of something eternal*! This is the vision of Descartes, and it is also mine. When the Greek mathematician – to take a simple example, the simplest example – when the Greek mathematician demonstrated some properties of numbers, the infinity of prime numbers, for example, when he proposed this he proposed something that did not exist before but that is eternal. It did not exists because before this demonstration no one even knew what a prime number was, and nobody knew what was the infinite, and so on. What is important to understand is that what we have here is an affirmation of some creation, some creation that once it is created is eternal – after this moment of time it is forever... it is forever, it is until the end of time, if you want.

This is the last possibility of the relationship of time and eternity. And it is a possibility with a long history – we find something like this in Plato as well, after all. It is, finally, the possibility of the existence of something eternal in time... *in time, but not in the mystic form.* Mysticism is a form of this possibility, but in its form this existence is a point, only a point, and it is a point that is not conceptual, not transmissible, not collective, finally. Philosophy, on the other hand, proposes that we have the possibility of creating something eternal, of creating a truth... and a truth which is rational, which is for all, and maybe a truth which is collective.

We stop here. Thank you.

6. Day Six

6.1 Lecture X

To finish with this question of the relationship between philosophy and time, I want to describe what must be the work of the philosopher, from the point of view of time. What is the concrete activity of thinking? Not the activity of writing a book, exams and so on, but the subjective activity inside the world as it is, in the direction of some effect of philosophy, other than knowledge. We have said that philosophy is not reducible to knowledge, and if philosophy is not reducible to knowledge, then the effect of philosophy cannot be reducible to the production of knowledge. It must be something like a challenge for humanity, a challenge of humanity. Maybe by the means of some knowledge, but that is not the goal.

So, what is the action of the philosopher in the direction of the present? I think that there is, first, a negative action, which is to resist the logic of places. Philosophy must resist the logic of places, which is – as I have explained – the fundamental logic of the world. And in every world there is always a tendency to construct some place for the philosopher, and this is particularly true in modern societies. And, certainly, there is pleasure and comfort in accepting such a place. And so the question of places is also a subjective question: on what condition can we accept to be in such a place *as a philosopher*? Concretely, today, this is the question of the relation that philosophy – and so philosophers – must maintain to the university, but not only to the university, there is also the relation to the media, and, sometimes, to even stranger places. For example, after my book

Ethics was published, I was invited by some bank to give a talk concerning the ethics of money – you can see now that it was not such a bad idea. I refused, naturally. I refused because – as you know – it is always a process: first you give one lecture in a bank concerning abstract considerations about the ethics of money, and they give you a lot of money, and after that.... To refuse is generally to refuse the first step, because if you accept the first step, then, it is easier to accept the second, and the third, and so on... and slowly, step by step, you become more and more corrupted. But you are not corrupted only by the money! Nor even by the fact that it is a bank! You become corrupted also by the very question of place, you become corrupted by the logic of places! This question of place, of a new place, of a good place, and so on, is a very important question.

It is interesting to consider the accusation against Socrates – Socrates was accused of corruption, as you all know. But this accusation is, in fact, a reversal of the truth. Why? Because it was precisely Socrates' actions which were directed against corruption, against a certain subjective corruption. To examine all things, to discuss the laws of the city, to have a new attitude, a new subjective figure, and so on, all that was an action against corruption by the world as it is. And so, the accusation of Socrates was something like a reversal of the truth – the truth is that it was Socrates who was against corruption, because he opposed a certain subjective corruption, which was the idea that to have a place, *a good place*, in the world as it is is the first imperative, *the only imperative*.

We have a very similar situation today, in fact: today too there exists the idea that the first imperative is to have a good place in this world. And to oppose this is the first action of the philosopher, certainly – the philosopher must reject this imperative, and the philosopher must resist the corruptive logic of places. And it is not easy, it is not at all easy. In fact, today it is maybe even more difficult because today there is also the temptation of the media – it is very tempting to be in the media, everyone likes to be in the media, after all, but it is a corruption. And, certainly, if you have written a book, and if you think that this book is important, that this book can have some real effects, you could say that it is important to be in the media, because without something like that the book will be ignored. And so it is not only a difficulty, but also a necessity, a necessity for the action of the philosophy at another level. This necessity makes the temptation constant, and so the possibility of corruption is constant.

But if you promote the book in the media, then the media will construct a figure of you. My figure, for example, is that of the extreme revolutionary philosopher. In the media there is the right, the center, the left, and then something beyond the left, something much more left than the left, and this position is my place. And when there is some question of politics, it is, in some sense, good if such a position exists, naturally. But, finally, we cannot accept this figure, we cannot accept to be a figure determined not by us but by the media. And so, it is a constant negotiation, and, finally, it is a constant negotiation with yourself, it is an intimate negotiation. For example, I have proposed to the media my conditions: I accept to be in the media if I am alone with the interviewer, face to face, and so no collective debates – collective debates on television are a spectacle and something very negative – and I want as a minimum 20 minutes – and 20 minutes in television is, as you know, an eternity. But when you say to them 'Okay, you want me? Perfect. Alone, on my own and for 20 minutes', the offer is no longer the same. But sometimes an offer exists under these conditions, and in such a case I accept. It is a simple example, but, certainly, the life of a philosopher today involves something like this: we must negotiate, we must calculate, we must think the relationship between freedom and constraint, we must think what exactly is the place of corruption, when corruption begins, we must think the relation, the balance, *the strategy* of how to approach the contradiction of the necessity of collective life and the beginning of corruption – all of that requires constant attention, constant thought.

All of this is a part of the general activity of the philosopher, because philosophy is not possible as a corrupted philosophy, it is not possible inside of the logic of place. It is not possible because the destiny of philosophy, if the philosopher accepts that sort of place, is to become a propagandist of power. And philosophy, finally, can assist the subjective transformation of some young philosophers into this figure, which is, in my conviction, not philosophical at all, but a destruction by corruption of the philosophical subjectivity. And so, in the direction of the present we have a negative action which is a resistance, a resistance to the logic of places... *and not only abstractly*. And, finally, you must, in some sense, accept something like a place, *but you must refuse....* It is a subjective problem.

In the direction of the present there is also a second action, which is to be in a relationship with new truth-processes. On this point I am classical, I am classical because the classical philosophers were of the idea that they must be connected to what exists in the form of newness in knowledge – in artistic creation, in politics, and so on. And philosophy, as you all know, must also refuse specialization, because it cannot be in just some narrow vision, in some small dimension of the contemporary world. And this too, finally, is a difficulty, because today specialization is a sort of law of activity, of thought, in all fields – we know that there is scientific specialization, technical specialization, but, finally, this law exists in all fields. The rule is that the relationship between philosophy and everything that has the possibility of creating something new, some new truth, must be as large as possible. It is my rule: you must have relation to political experience, to artistic creations, to new scientific theories, and so on. And why? Because the great task of philosophy is to create a new concept of Truth, a Truth adequate to the contemporary truths. And so, naturally, if you are absolutely outside of these creations this task is impossible. There is something like an encyclopedic desire of the philosopher – the philosopher must know everything.

This was the case for classical philosophers until Hegel, probably. Maybe Hegel was the last to know everything.... It is why he has written an *Aesthetics*, a *Logic*, a *Phenomenology*, a *Philosophy of Right*, a *Philosophy of Nature*, and so on. Probably it is impossible to know everything, but to know the sites where the possibility of something new exists is an imperative. Maybe it is not completely possible, *but it's a rule, it's a rule*. Philosophy is without specialization... *it must be without specialization*. I am absolutely opposed to some academic definitions like philosophy of mathematics, philosophy of algebra, philosophy of music, philosophy of cinema, philosophy of politics, and so on. All of these are disciplines, but none are philosophy, they are all different parts of scholasticism.

Philosophy can exist! But the existence of philosophy has conditions, and these conditions are precisely the living processes of truths. Maybe we do not yet know where these living processes of truth are in our present. In the 17th century, for example, certainly the most important living process of truth was science, but that is not always the case. For example, at the core of the 19th century the fields for the creation of new truths were art and politics. We cannot decide in advance where these places of real creation, these places where something new may emerge, will be in our time. And so, we must have a sort of general experience, a general knowledge, a general awareness of all of the conditions, and we must search. But to search we have to know something. After all, we wouldn't even understand what is a new creation in the field of mathematics, for example, if we knew nothing of mathematics – if we knew nothing of mathematics we wouldn't even be able to see the truth, the process of a truth. The philosopher himself does not create truths – he is not a scientist, ne is not an artist, and so on – but he must be in a relationship with these conditions, he must know them, he must know the places where the possibility of some new truth exists. And so, when I propose that philosophy is conditioned – by science, art, love, and politics, it is a minimal list – this is also a proposition about the activity of the philosopher in the direction of the present. This determination, this sort of geography of truth, if you want, is necessarily a condition for being a philosopher.

So we have two actions in the direction of the present: first, the philosopher must resist corruption, and second, the philosopher must have a minimal knowledge concerning the different fields of thought. And both of these very difficult tasks, certainly... – it is very difficult to be a philosopher. One day, in fact, I would like to write a small book under the title '*The Conditions for Being a Philosopher*'. And why? Why is this important? Why must we clarify these conditions? Because, today, *everybody is a philosopher,* and so there is even something like the corruption of the name itself. Naturally my vision is that one day everyone will be a philosopher, certainly – it is my vision of communism, if you want: *everybody is a philosopher*! But to create the conditions for that sort of collective organization we must first refuse the corruption of this name, and so we must clarify the conditions. If there are no conditions for being a philosopher, then, certainly, everybody is already a philosopher. We must clarify what is philosophy, and we must resurrect the idea of philosophy, and we must, finally, oppose the corruption of philosophy by the world as it is. And so, I repeat: philosophy must resist corruption and it must desire knowledge of all the different possibilities concerning new truths. These are the actions of the philosopher in the direction of the present.

In the direction of the past there are also two different actions. The first is that we must assume the complete history of philosophy – I have already proposed the proposition. The philosophical present is as big as all of its past, and it is *because philosophy assumes all of the past that philosophy can propose a real future* – a future which is as great as the past, and not only a tomorrow. We must assume the complete history of philosophy, but not strictly in the form of an analytical knowledge of this history.

But how can we assume the complete history of philosophy? We can assume it by the proposition of *a new interpretation of this past*. And so, this assumption is not purely a question of a historical knowledge of philosophy. Rather, we must *resurrect* the great philosophers *in our present*. And this is very problematic, because, naturally, the history of philosophy is a matter for scholasticism – the reduction of philosophy to the history of philosophy is scholasticism, in fact. If we reduce philosophy to the history of philosophy, then we have reduced philosophy to a knowledge, and so the condition for being a philosopher is just a knowledge of the history philosophy. And, in fact, this is precisely the definition of the philosopher within the field of academic studies: the philosopher is the one who knows philosophy, the one who knows the history of philosophy. But what is philosophy if the philosopher is reduced to merely knowing the history of philosophy? And if the conditions for being a philosopher are not reduced to this scholastic knowledge, then what is it that a philosopher does? The philosopher creates philosophy! And so, if you wish to preserve the creative dimension of philosophy, then you must assume the complete history of philosophy, but assume it in the name of the present and, finally, in the name of the future! And what is this assumption? It is precisely *a new interpretation of the past*!

This is the first action of the philosopher in the direction of the past: the philosopher must propose new interpretations of Plato, Hegel, of Wittgenstein, and so on. The second is a relationship to the truths of the past. And so, philosophy must engage with the complete history of artistic creation, the complete history of mathematics, and so on. Why? Because to be in a relationship with new truths – as we have already said – implies that you know something concerning old truths. After all, in every field invention there is some relation between the old and the new. And so a philosopher must be in a relationship with the truths of the past, precisely because this is the condition for engaging new interpretations in the present. We return, therefore, to the encyclopedic question: is it possible to know, or to be in relationship with, so many truths, the truths of all the ancient worlds, and so on?

Certainly this is an enormous task, and maybe an impossible task, and so every philosopher must make choices: he must choose to be more in Greek tragedy than Japanese theatre, for example, or more in algebra than topology, and so on. This action, therefore, always has a biographical dimension – there is some choice, some subjective choice, and this choice is ultimately biographical. We can name this the culture of the philosopher. And so, of each philosopher we can ask what is his culture, what conditions his thought, and so on. And this resurrection of past truths – with its subjective element – has great consequences, consequences that orient the philosophical conception of Truth. We cannot escape this point. And so, for the second time we must affirm the particular subjective existence of a philosopher, because there is a culture, a specific culture of a philosopher – what he has read, what he has loved, what sorts of truths are in his subjectivity, and so on. That is the activity of the philosopher in the direction of the past.

Finally, in the direction of the future the action of the philosopher is to propose a new concept of Truth. The philosopher proposes this concept *for the future, in the present, and on the basis of a new interpretation of the past.* But why must we propose a *new concept of Truth*? After all, can we not simply affirm that the old ideas are good? And if we can, then why work to create a *new conception of Truth*? Is this not the task of philosophy from the beginning? And has philosophy not been successful? Finally, why is it that we must do something like this *after Plato, after Descartes, after Hegel*, and so on? We must because philosophy is conditioned! Philosophy is not reducible to its proper history! And philosophy always begins... philosophy always begins *because it is conditioned*, and these conditions change. They change because over time we create new truths in art, in science, in politics, in love.... And so philosophy must continually examine new truths, it must examine them to see whether they introduce or do not introduce something new into the concept of Truth.

You cannot explain what is a Truth in a void, and you cannot explain it only in reference to the history of philosophy, and, finally, you cannot construct Truth in such conditions either! A new Truth is possible *only if there exist new truths*! And the history of truths is a living history, and not a pure repetition. We can take a very simple example. During many centuries the idea of truth in the field of painting was imitation – the imitation of nature, for example – and so the question of art was always something like what is the proper from of imitation, what to imitate, what is the essence of something, and so on. And, naturally, over the course of this great history we have many different propositions, different philosophical propositions, in the field of aesthetics. But from Plato until the middle of the 19th

century there was a common affirmation that the goal of painting is some form of mimesis, some form of imitation. And from this affirmation we have derived many question, many very interesting questions, many concepts and so on: what is imitation, is imitation transformation, must imitation be transformation, what is to be imitated, what is the essence, and so on. Out of this, out of this entire history of propositions, considerations, concepts and so on, we have constituted a very complex, and very subtle field of aesthetics.

But across this entire history – at least until the 19th century – the common idea is that an artistic truth in painting, for instance, is a question of imitation, and after that a question of the elaboration or transformation of some form of this idea. Today we cannot say the same. A philosopher today cannot say that the very essence of painting – or artistic creation, more generally – is imitation. We know that there exist artistic possibilities which are not only not imitation, but the explicit goal of which is to destroy imitation itself, to create something which is not under the law of imitation, something that *cannot be* under the law of imitation.

From the end of the 19th century it has become completely clear that the history of the plastic arts – of painting first, but after painting other forms as well – is not in the field of imitation. And philosophy, as a result of this change, must begin constructing a new concept of Truth – it must construct a new concept of Truth because the truth of one field can no longer be what it was.

After the 19th century, therefore, we had to begin thinking about what is art – and this is still a fundamental problem in the field of contemporary aesthetics. And you must understand that this problem concern things beyond artistic production – it concerns art, naturally, but it also concerns some things which are outside of art. It is not only a technical problem, but also, finally, an ontological problem – what is the being of art? And this question is still very much open. Naturally, if the philosophy speaks about art only across the history of philosophy – and so, only across various forms of imitation – then philosophy cannot possibly produce a complete conception of Truth, which would be appropriate to our present. It is clear: philosophy must begin again, it must again construct a new concept of Truth – it must, because the old concept is now necessarily incomplete. We must understand that such a passage – a passage from one conception of truth in art to another – is not a passage from a falsity to a truth, but the passage from a truth under some conditions to a truth under other conditions. And, generally, it is like this across all creation in the philosophical field.

And so, in the direction of the future we maintain that the philosophical action is to propose a new concept of Truth. In fact, we can justify this point. Philosophy is conditioned, and so if there is a change in these conditions then philosophy must react. And, as we all perfectly know, across history there are new truths in all fields. I took the example of art, and the function of imitation in painting, but we could just as well have taken the example of politics. We know that during the 19th century there was a great transformation in the very idea of what is politics – it is not the same after the French Revolution, after the Paris Commune, after Marxism, and so on, as it was before. For long sequences of history politics was reduced to the questions of what is a good state, what is a good power, or what is the best power. And the philosophical question of political truth was to find, or to propose, a new concept of truth in the field of politics, its task was to prescribe the conditions and the very nature of good power, of good government. Today we cannot say something like that, since today the question of politics is much more radical. For example, a new politics cannot be completely in the economy of the present world, since we must destroy some parts of capitalism, we must organize the power of collectivity in a new manner, and so on. Political truth today cannot be reduced to the classical question of what is good power. Maybe, for example, the true idea of politics today is an orientation of history in the direction of the abolition of the question of power, or the end of the state. In fact, this was Marx's idea: Marx's question was not what is a good power, but precisely whether something like a separate state is really necessary. This is just an example, a very brief example. The point that we must understand is that if there is change in the conditions, a change in the situation, then the proposition of a Truth adequate to out time cannot be a pure repetition.

A particularly important question has been the transformation of the question of the truth concerning the infinite. For many centuries the question of the infinite was the question of God – there was no distinction between the question of the infinite and the question of God. And it is only by the immanent transformation of mathematics that the question of the infinite becomes a question completely separate from the theological question of God. We could examine this transformation in great detail, but what is important for us to understand is that today if we speak of the infinite, of the truth of the infinite, we are not restricted to the theological field, and, in consequence, to its conception of the infinite. But this was the case for Descartes, and even for Leibniz, both of whom were great mathematicians. And so, if there is some relationship between truth and infinite, the philosopher today can and must examine this question in many fields, and not only in relation to the potency of God. And, it is clear that with this possibility philosophy can arrive at different conclusions, at different conceptions of Truth. And why is this possible? It is possible solely because of advances in mathematics!

And so we must resist and we must know many things, we must propose a new interpretation of the complete history of philosophy and we must be in relationship to new truths, and, finally, we must propose a new conception of what is a Truth. And a new conception of Truth is also a new conception of being, a new conception of existence, a new conception of event and subject, and so on. That is the landscape of the life of the philosopher – that is the final landscape of our lives.

We can now return to the idea of the difference between two possible orientations of philosophy - beginning in being and beginning in existence. We have this difference in the difference between my two books: *Being and Event* and *Logics of Worlds*. The difference between them functions for us here only as an example of the very general difference which we can observe in books of many philosophers, across its entire history.

As I have already said, the fundamental question of *Being and Event* was to find an answer to the question of the being of a truth, and so its logic is the logic of being. And I have explained – and you have a text concerning this – that my answer to this question is that the being of truth is a generic subset of the situation. That is, the being of a truth is a part of the situation not reducible to a name or predicate that exists in the situation. And so the being of a truth has no identity in the situation, no name, no knowledge, it is outside the language of the situation – in the language of the situation we have no name for that sort of generic subset. And so a generic subset is inside of the situation – it is not outside – but, in some sense, it is not inside the situation, because it is not identifiable by the state of the situation itself. The generic subset, then, is present in the situation, but it is also absent – it is a presence in the form of absence.

This was, in fact, Marx's conception of the working class, of the proletariat: the proletariat is a subset of the society, but a subset which has no right to exist in the society as it is in the 19th century. And so, it's a subset of political existence but without any right, without any name, without any knowledge or recognition. And so the proletariat is, in some sense, nothing, but this nothing is not non-being, this nothing is, in some sense, something – we return to the beginning with Socrates, we return to the point where thing and nothing are the same. In some sense the generic subset is something like that: a generic subset is a reality, you can observe that sort of existence, but there is no identity, no knowledge, no representation, and so it's a mixture of presence and absence.

And you understand why something like that can be of universal value? It can be of universal value precisely because it is something that is within a situation but not completely prescribed by the situation, it is the unknown of the situation – it is without name, and so on – and so it is also a possibility for another world. For Marx, for example, it is clear: for Marx the working class exists, but has no place in the society, no representation, no specific representation, it has nothing, finally, it is something like pure existence with no place. And you know it is interesting that Marx named the proletariat 'the generic form of humanity' – the name generic is here in the texts of Marx. And Marx's idea – his idea of universality – is that the working class, since it has no place, can create a world without place.

This passage involved the destruction of the world of different classes, of different places, and so on, and it is the possibility of a world of complete equality, which is precisely a world without strict determination by social place. And for Marx, the proletariat are the agents of this passage, they are the agents precisely because they are the generic subset of society, and their political organization would be in the direction of a society without places, a society without distinctions or differentiations, a society of equality. The most important point is that Marxism made it possible to hope for and to think a society without place, society of justice, *precisely because in our society there exists something generic* – in an oppressed form, naturally, but it exists.

That was my fundamental question in *Being and Event* – to identify the being of a truth as a generic subset. And the generic set is not limited to the political field, not at all. We can absolutely give examples of what is a generic subset in all fields of creativity. For example, in artistic creation, the point is always that the new truth is possible because you displace or you modify the distinction between what is form and what is not a from – between what is accepted as a form, and what is not accepted, what is considered un-formed. And the displacement of this limit is always the possibility of a new artistic field wherein the notion of form is completely altered. In fact between the 19th century and the last century we have a revolution, an artistic revolution in music, in painting, and so on, which were brutal displacements of what is accepted as a form and what is not. Today this situation is much more complex, naturally. And we can identify such a shift the moment that we have a generic set, which is to say, the moment we have something which is not recognized as an aesthetic form by the knowledge of the situation but which is functioning as an aesthetic form. In this sense it is the same as with the proletariat, who cannot be recognized but can become a political agent.

Finally, my goal was to propose that the being of truth is a generic subset, and after that to give a proof that generic subsets exist. There were, of course, objections to this proposition, and so I had to prove the generic subset, I had to prove that it is something coherent, that it has being, and that it can exist. First I gave a mathematical proof: at this completely abstract level we can prove that there is a generic subset, because we can construct and understand the subset of a set which is generic – which has no name, no predicate, no specific properties, which is, if you want, anonymous, in a sense. Naturally, this was only possible because the notion of generic set had been introduced into the field of mathematics. And so the generic is also an example of the possibility of a modification in one condition effecting another field of creativity. The technicalities of Cohen's theorem are not important for us here, what is important is the simple fact that the creation of the notion of generic set in the beginning of the 60's of the last century is the strict condition for me to propose a new conception of the being of truth. And so it is also an absolutely clear proof of the relationship between the conditions and the conceptual world of philosophy.

So that was my work in *Being and Event*. What was my work in *Logics of Worlds*? The question this time was not the being of truth, but its form of existence. We had the generic set, but that is only the ontological form of truth, and so the question that remained was whether that sort of thing can exist in a real world – we know that to exist is not the same as to be. The proof that something has being is, naturally, not at all already the proof that it exists. In fact this has been at the heart of all the problems of proving God's existence: the proof of the existence of God was primarily under the law of the determination of his being – His being was the proof of His existence. Again we have here the problem of the relationship between being and existence. Naturally, to prove the existence of God you must first define God – how can you prove the existence of something without a prior definition? It's impossible, clearly. And so, first you must define God and after that there follows a definition of the existence of such a Being. But the entire problem was that this existence was an existence not of this world, and the demonstration of the existence of God could not be the demonstration of the existence of God in a world. And the problem, then, was what sort of sort of existence is it if it is not in a world? Or: what do we really prove when we prove the existence of God? Or even: if God does not exist in a world, where then is the existence of God? You understand – of course – that God is the point where being and existence do not differ. Finally, the poofs of God's existence – even Descartes' – are ontological proofs, they are proofs which affirm that God is a being which necessarily exists, and so He exists! But that is not a proof! And there is a very strong critique of Descartes' argument in Kant, because, as he says, we cannot define existence in the case of God in another manner than to define His being – the definition of the being of God is clearly the definition of the existence of God – and so there can be no proof of existence. If you assume the being of God, if you assume that God is, you assume that God exists – God is not an object of this world, and to exist is to be an object of a concrete world. This, finally, was a purely philosophical question....

And so the difficulty with truth is that when we define its being – for example, as a generic subset – this cannot give us direct proof of its existence in a world. And so we need a second process, a second argument, which demonstrates that this sort of being can exist in a world. There is no direct passage from being to existence – proof of existence is not an ontological proof... because truth is not God, after all. And so we must demonstrate that truths exist, that they exist in concrete worlds, we must demonstrate that something like an immanent exception to the laws of a world can exist in the world.

The difficulty in *Being and Event was at the end* – the difficulty was to demonstrate that truths can be conceived in the form of a generic subset. The difficulty of *Logics of World* was *at the beginning* – the difficulty was to show how a truth can exist in a world. And so, it was first necessary to define a world – after all, how could you give a proof of the possibility of something's existence in a world, before you define existence? And if existence is existence in a world, and not in general, you must define what a world is, what a place where some being exists is. With such a problem, we are really in philosophy.

And you must see now why it is impossible to give a proof of the existence of God? It is impossible because there is no place for that sort of existence, there is no place for God other than God Himself... of Herself, or Itself – maybe God is a Woman, maybe He is a man, *but He is not an object, He cannot be an object of a world.* God is beyond every world – we cannot conceive of a world for God. And so existence in a world cannot be existence in general, because existence in general cannot be properly distinguished from being – this is the point, and so we need to prove the existence of truths *in a concrete world*, and *not in general*!

And so to have a real difference between being and existence you need a concept of world, a world defined as a space where some things can exist. And so in *Logics of Worlds* the most important concept was not directly involved with the question of truth, but with the question of world: it is was absolutely necessary to define a world, because otherwise it would be impossible to have a rigorous distinction between being and existence.

We can propose that a possible definition of God is precisely that God is a being in which we cannot distinguish being and existence – we cannot distinguish them because God has no place to exist. Finally, *God exists because God is.* We return always to this point, because it is the definition of God. It is the definition of the metaphysical God, not of the Greek Gods – the Greek Gods have a place, they are on Mount Olympus, in the mountains, or here, for example, in Saas-Fee, in the snow, and they exist, they are men or women, and they have many strange stories, monsters, and so on. The Greek gods, finally, are not at all metaphysical Gods, they are the gods of stories, of mythology, and they are, in some sense, good gods. The metaphysical God, on the other hand, is fundamentally the question of the One, He is the emergence of the question of the One: the One who is infinite, the One the nature of whose being is to exist, and the One who is alone, utterly alone. The Greek gods, on the other hand are not infinite, but absolute finite, and they exists in a world, and, finally, they are certainly not alone.

With the invention of the metaphysical God – of the being which is One and infinite, and which exists by necessity – what is interesting it to give a proof that with the metaphysical God we abolish the distinction between being and existence. And, probably, the progressive failure of classical metaphysics begins when it becomes impossible to fuse, or to put into one, being and existence. And this became impossible because of the transformation of the concept of the infinite, absolutely: *the God of metaphysics is dead because the infinite itself cannot unify being and existence.* The classical conception was that being and existence are the same in God because God is infinite – this was the solution. In the theological infinite the One of God is also His existence, but with the transformation of the infinite this was no longer possible.

With this problem we are at what Heidegger and many others have called the end of classical metaphysics, which is precisely the end of the possibility of that sort of God. Maybe it is possible to create another God, or to prove the existence of another God in some place, but the metaphysical God after the transformation of the infinite – which made impossible the fusion of being and existence – Himself became impossible. And so we must affirm the distinction between being and existence, and this distinction is, naturally, possible only if we have a place *for existence.* And so we must define what a world is. And this, finally, is why the title of the second book – which assumes the problem of the existence of truths – is not *Being and Event,* but *Logics of Worlds.* As a closure to all this, I shall read to you a second text.

This text is also a lecture, and it is, I believe, a clear presentation of the question of what is a world and what is existence. The title of the text is *Towards a New Concept of Existence* – it is a clear title. I will read to you a small part of the text, and after that you shall have the text.

> ""What is a thing?" It is the title of a famous Heidegger essay. What is a thing as some thing which is without any determination of its being, except precisely being as such? We can speak of an object of the world. We can distinguish it in the world by its properties or predicates. In fact, we can experience the complex network of identities and differences by which this object is clearly not identical to another object of the same world. But a thing is not an object."

Just as a commentary: I propose to inscribe the distinction between being and existence in the distinction between a thing, a pure thing, and an object.

> "A thing is not yet an object. Like the hero of the great novel by Robert Musil, a thing is something without qualities. We must think of the thing before its objectivation in a precise world.
>
> The Thing is... . That is this form of being which certainly is after the indifference of nothingness, but also before the qualitative difference of object. We must formalize the concept of "thing" between, on the one hand, the absolute priority of

> nothingness and, on the other hand, the complexity of objects. A thing is always the pre-objective basis of objectivity. And that is the reason for which a thing is nothing other than a multiplicity. Not a multiplicity of objects, not a system of qualities, a network of differences, but a multiplicity of multiplicities, and a multiplicity of multiplicities of multiplicities. And so on. Is there an end to that sort of "dissemination," to speak like Jacques Derrida? Yes, there is an end point. But this end point is not a primitive object, or an atomic component, it is not a form of the One. The end point is of necessity also a multiplicity. The multiplicity which is the multiplicity of no multiplicity at all, the thing which is also no-thing: the void, the empty multiplicity, the empty set. If a thing is between indifference and difference, nothingness and objectivity, it is because a pure multiplicity is composed of the void. The multiple as such has to do with difference and pre-objectivity. The void has to do with indifference and complete lack of object."

All that was a summary of the fundamental ontology of *Being and Event*: under the name of thing I presented the name of being, which is just after nothingness, in the form of the void, and which is just before existence, in the form of objectivity. The determination of the thing is the determination of being, and it is a determination without qualities, because it is not in a concrete world. And so it is something between the pure indifference of nothingness – in nothingness we cannot find a difference, naturally, because there is nothing – and objectivity, in which we have differences, which are the differences of objects. A thing, therefore, is something between nothingness and objectivity, and it is something that, in some sense, is composed of nothing, because it is composed of the void, which is the first set, the empty set. After this, the compositions of the empty set, the primitive set, create all possible forms of being.

Now I will go to the question of the world.

"Let us suppose now that we have a pure multiplicity, a thing, which can be formalized as a set. We want to understand what is exactly the appearing, or being-there, of this thing, in a determinate world. The idea is that when the thing, or the set, is localized in a world, it is because the elements of the set are inscribed in a completely new evaluation of their identities. It becomes possible to say that this element, for instance x, is more or less identical to another element, for instance y. In classical ontology, there are only two possibilities: either x is the same as y, or x is not at all identical to y. You have either strict identity, or difference. By contrast, in a concrete world as a place for being-there of multiplicities, we have a great variety of possibilities. A thing can be very similar to another, or similar in some ways and different in others, or a little identical to, or very identical but not really the same, and so on. So every element of a thing can be related to others by what we shall name: a degree of identity. The fundamental characteristic of a world is the distribution of that sort of degrees to all multiplicities which appear in this world.

So, in the very concept of appearing, or of being-there, or of a world, we have two things. We have first a system of degrees, with an elementary structure which authorizes the comparison of

> degrees. We must be able to observe that this thing
> is more identical to this other thing than to that
> third thing. So the degrees certainly have the
> formal structure of an order. They admit, maybe
> within certain limits, the "more" and the "less.""

So you see, the world is the introduction of the qualitative dimension, of the possible qualitative dimension of the thing. And this qualitative dimension progressively determines the thing through differences, identities, nuances and so on, in short, through the deployment of qualitative determination, and transforms the pure thing into an object of the world. And an object is precisely the appearance of a thing in the form of some qualitative determination, which is always a comparison between that form of quality and another quality in the same world.

> "This structure is the rational disposition of the
> infinite shades of a concrete world. I name the
> ordinal organization of the degrees of identities:
> the transcendental of the world."

This is another important concept. The transcendental of the world is the structure which creates the possibility of the world to be a place where we have qualitative differences between different things. And so it is the condition of possibility for the properties of things, and when things come to have properties then they are something more than things, they become objects. They are not objects by themselves, they are objects because they appear – the thing appears in a world with a determinate transcendental.

> "Second of all, we have a relationship between the
> things (the multiplicities) and the degrees of
> identities. That is precisely the meaning of being-

in-a-world for a thing. With these two
determinations we have the meaning of the
becoming object of the thing."

After that there is a clear explanation and an example of how
this machinery works. And so I will conclude with existence.

"We have here a profound and difficult
understanding of what happens to a multiplicity
when it really appears in a world, or when it is not
merely reducible to its pure immanent
composition. The appearing multiplicity must be
understood as a very complex network of degrees
of identity between its elements, parts and atoms.
We have to take care of the logic of its qualities,
and not only the mathematics of its extension. We
must think, beyond its pure being, of something
like an existential intensity.

There I have said it: existence, existential. I am
finally under the title of my lecture. What is the
process of definition of existence, in the
transcendental framework of appearing, or being-
there?"

So, how can we define existence in a world, under all of these
conditions?

"I give you immediately my conclusion: Existence
is the name for the value of the identity function
when it is applied to one and the same element. It
is, so to speak, the measure of the identity of a
thing to itself.

Given a world and an identity function having its
values in the transcendental of this world, we will

call "existence" of a being that appears in this
world, the transcendental degree assigned to the
identity of this being to itself. Thus defined,
existence is not a category of being (in
mathematics), it is a category of appearing (in
logic). In particular, "to exist" has no sense in
itself."

This is precisely the difference between an object and a God.

"According to an intuition of Sartre's, "to exist"
can only be said relatively to a world. In effect,
existence is a transcendental degree which
indicates the intensity of appearance of a
multiplicity in a determined world, and this
intensity is in no way prescribed by the pure
multiple composition of the being in
consideration.

We can apply to existence the formal remarks of
the previous part of my lecture. If, for instance, the
degree of identity of a thing to itself is the
maximal degree, we can say that the thing exists in
the world without any limitation. The multiplicity,
in this world, completely affirms its own identity.
Symmetrically, if the degree of identity of a thing
to itself is the minimal degree, we can say that this
thing does not exist in this world. The thing is in
the world, but with an intensity which is equal to
zero. So we can say that its existence is a non-
existence. We have here a striking example of the
distinction between being and existence. The thing
is in the world, but its appearance in the world is
the destruction of its identity. So the being-there
of this being is to be the inexistent of the world.

> The theory of the inexistent of a world is very
> important. I have shown that the situation of the
> inexistent is fundamental in Jacques Derrida's
> work."

To conclude all of this, I will make one just a final comment. All of the details of this structure can be very complex, certainly, but the general idea is very simple, in some sense. The world is a place, which, as a place, is also a distribution of differences, differences concerning the composition of objects, differences with other objects, detailed differences. We are here not in a logic where there is a strict opposition between difference and identity, but one where there are degrees of intensities of difference – things can be identical, they can be very different, not very different, and so on.

We can apply this to the object itself: an object can be different not only from another object, but also from itself. This is the most important point to understand. In being we have the principle of identity: a thing is identical to itself – this is the law of being, it is the oldest law of being, it is the law we find in Parmenides: being is identical to being. And so the thing is identical to itself. But in appearance this is not the case, because a being affirms its identity as an object in a different manner. Naturally something can appear brilliantly in a world, or appear weakly, and so we have many degrees of appearance for the same thing, and if the thing appears completely then it completely affirms its identity in the world. In such a case we can say that the thing is completely here, completely in the world. But if a thing is in the world very differently from itself, if its identity with itself is not strong in this world, then it has a weak existence. And so we have two possibilities: the thing is in the world but does not really appear in the world because it is completely different from itself, or a thing appears in the world completely, and so it is completely identical to itself, in which case its difference with itself is negative.

And this, finally, is why a world is always a distribution of places: the dominant places are those where identities are completely affirmed, and the dominated are places where the thing is reduced to a very poor appearance, a very poor identity with itself. *Every world is a distribution of places* – the places can be very different or the places can be very similar. It depends on what? It depends only on the distribution of the transcendental degrees to the thing, and so it's a dependence on the transcendental of the world.

And so, if you want to change the distribution of places, what you want, finally, is to destroy the world. Why? Because if the world is the transcendental of the distribution of degrees of identity, then to change the place is to change the degrees of identity. More fundamentally, it is for something to pass from a poor identity to itself to a strong degree of identity to itself. And this is why the question of the inexistent is so important in an event: we can define an event in a world as a brutal change of the degree of appearance of some part of the world. This was also the fundamental idea of Marx: the working class was nothing, but it can become everything, *it can be everything*.... In our terminology: the appearance of the working class has a very low degree of existence in one world, but thought political action we can force a very strong degree of identity to itself. And how? Precisely by the mediation of its proper organization.

There is, then, a strong relationship between the idea of the refusal of places and the idea of something like the destruction of the world itself, the name of which in Marxism is revolution. Revolution is precisely the passage from one transcendental of the world to another transcendental of the world, a passage by which the distribution of differences and so the distribution of places is completely changed. But all of this is not in the law of being, because across all of that multiplicities are multiplicities, and things are things. It is a change at the level of appearance, it is a complete transformation of appearance, that is, it is a change in the manner in which something is or exists in the world. This is why the question of an event is not only an ontological question – a question of the rupture of repetition – but also an existential question, because it is a change of the transcendental of the world.

Okay, my slave...I give you the text... – you have a bad place.

6.2 Discussion II

There are many questions, and so it will be difficult to answer all
of them in the short time that we have. First, two questions
concerning the notion of exception, immanent exception. The
first question is a question from Nico.

*Question 1: When you discussed great exceptions in our lives –
experiences which are not reducible – how is this different from
19th century visions of the sublime? Specifically in the
metaphysical sense.*

[Badiou]: The notion of the sublime is introduced by Kant, and
some others, at the beginning of the 19th century, to describe a
specific affect. The sublime is a form, a subjective form, of the
effect on consciousness of the presence of some aspects, some
dimensions or facts in the world. And so, certainly there is a
relation between the sublime in this sense and the event, as a
form of exception, because the affect of the sublime is in
relationship to some transformations, some extraordinary fact of
nature – disaster, catastrophe, for example – and also
revolutions. There is for Kant something sublime in the French
Revolution. By some aspects the French Revolution was horrible
for Kant, but it was sublime. And so a horrible thing can also be
sublime. And so, I agree with you, the sublime is really a part of
the slow construction of the concept of the event during all of
the 19th century and after. And the concept of event is not at all
mine: many philosophers, many contemporary philosophers –
Deleuze, for example – have spoken about and proposed some
concept of event. And, certainly, the description by Kant and

others of the sublime is something on the way to the conception of what is a rupture, and the implications of this for a subjectivity in front of a rupture, in front of a revolution, a disaster, a natural phenomenon, and so on.

The second question is a question of this man [Lionel, the translator].

Question 2: What are the possible concrete ethical implications of your concept of immanent exception?

[Badiou]: For me the fundamental subjective dimension of an immanent exception is the possibility to participate in its construction, because that sort of exception is always a possibility, a subjective possibility. An event is not by itself the birth of a truth, the truth must be constructed in a long process, and an event is, finally, just the creation of a possibility. We must understand this point: an event is not the creation of a new thing, but the creation of a new possibility, it is something like the opening of a new possibility, a possibility not visible in the situation becomes visible by the event. And this is very clear in a political event: it opens the possibility of a new sequence of history because it opens the possibility of something that was impossible, something that was not presented as a possibility. For example, in France before 1789 there was no one speaking about power without a king, or something like that – *this possibility, in fact, does not exist before 1789.* And even during the beginning of the revolutionary sequence this possibility does not exist! At the beginning of the revolution Robespierre himself is not a republican but a monarchist. An event – its minimal, but true definition – is the production of a possibility.

And after an event, or because of an event, we have the possibility to realize a new possibility. And this is, finally, why being inside the realization of a new possibility is always a subjective possibility. *And this is the beginning of the ethical question.*

The ethical question is the question of participation, of the decision to participate, in the realization of a new possibility, *and to continue*, to continue.... *Participation is not only a question of being in the great moment,* in the great evental moment, with passion and so on, *but of continuing, of continuing!* And so there are *two* ethical commitments: first, to be engaged by the event, but after that there is fidelity, which is something else, which is something else.... Everybody knows the passion of many people for the event in '68, or in the beginning of the French Revolution, but to continue is something else, it is really something else... and something difficult.

The definition of what is the fidelity to some event is step by step, it is step by step, and it becomes more complex, more difficult. At the beginning it is simple, it is enthusiasm, but with time it is much more difficult. And so we have two ethical questions: first the question of engagement and after that the question of continuation.

Now there is a group of questions concerning event, fidelity and truth, in sequence. First, a question of Alejandro.

Question 3: If truth is the result of successive choices that produce something new other than knowledge. How is this related to and different from Lacan's analysts discourse?

[Badiou]: There is naturally – and this is why the question is a good question – something similar between my description of the process of a truth and the position of analytic discourse, in fact, in the very description of the cure. Lacan explained that the analytical process is a process in which successive determinations, successive choices, create a situation in which something like a truth of the subject appears, the truth of the subject in the sense of something of the real of the subject. And it is by means that are symbolic means, and by imaginary means as well, that we proceed – if the analytical process is effective – in the direction of something which is the point of the real, the real of the subject. All that is similar. But the analytic discourse is about the real of an individual subject and so it is much more the revelation of something like the truth of the subject, than the creation of a new truth. And there is always something from the past which determines this truth – do not forget that psychoanalysis is a theory of the origin of subjectivity. And so, when we have to confront our real – in the psychoanalytic cure – it is always, in some sense, that we have to confront something real of our profound past. There is a formal identity between the two processes, but I think that, finally... – it is not exactly a contradiction, but – it is not the same thing because the position of truth is not the same, the position of truth is not the same. Maybe... maybe the analytic process is a process of something like revelation, of something that was there already – it is the concept of the unconscious, after all, and my vision of the subject is not that the subject is unconscious. But I do not speak of individual subjects, I speak of the anonymous subject, the collective subject, of artistic subjectivity, and so on.

The next question is from Josephine.

Question 4: What is the ontology of the event, the ontology of the cut? A decision? Or is an event an imposition? If it's a decision, then the pre-subject already desires the event itself, perhaps?

[Badiou]: I think that we must assume that an event is something like an imposition, and not the result of a desire, or of a decision. As such an event is of objective nature, it's not an object but it is something objective, because it is the point of the real of the situation. My demonstration was, precisely, that an event is, finally, something composed with elements of the situation – it is not like a miracle, which comes from outside, but an *immanent* exception. An event is composed of elements of the situation, but is not the result of the situation, because if it were the result of a situation it would not be an event but an extension, and there would be no decision, finally. And so, *in some sense* there is something to the event which comes from outside, for us – it's true, in some sense.

And an *event is*, in some sense, an imposition, but it is the imposition of a new possibility, and it's not an imposition in the sense of something oppressive, something which would force us to do something. It's a proposition, a proposition... an event is the proposition of a new possibility. And we can refuse this possibility, naturally – we can refuse it, we can say no. It is exactly as when you encounter somebody and there is something very important, something new, and so on, but, finally, you to decide not to change your life, you can decide to stay in the past. An event can be a temptation... and an event is a temptation, in fact: it is a temptation to be engaged, to be transformed, to do something new. But a temptation is also a temptation to refuse the temptation. Generally ethics is said to be a refusal of temptation, but my ethics is to accept the temptation, and not to refuse it – the temptation of the event must be accepted.... But there is a risk, there is always a risk.... And maybe there are good reasons to refuse... to refuse the evental proposition. There are good reasons: it's not practical, it's not useful, it's not possible, things are good, things are okay, and so on and so on. – And these good reasons are from inside of the world as it is, from inside the objective knowledge of the situation. And in this sense it always the same problem: you can demonstrate by good reason in the situation that this event is risky, that we don't really know the consequences, that even if the situation must change this change is not immediately good, that it is difficult, that it cannot be changed, that the situation cannot be different, and so on and so on.

There is a form of imposition in the event, but it is not a determination, it is the imposition of a new possibility, it is not an oppression, it is a freedom, finally. The only necessity is the necessity of a choice – it is the imposition of a choice. If there is an event we must accept or refuse the new possibility.

The question of Christof is next.

Question 4: What happens to the generic set of a localized event as time passes? Does it decay? Does it become untrue? Can its original truth be retrospectively denied?

[Badiou]: It is a real question to ask: if a truth, if the being of a truth is something like a subset of a world, of a situation, how can this subset exist when the world is changed, when the situation is another situation? The solution – which is a difficult one, but which is the solution – is precisely that the subset is generic, and a generic subset can be included in another world precisely because it is generic. A generic subset is a subset that is not really in the explicit composition of the situation itself – there is no name, there is no knowledge – and so the subset is quasi universal, in some sense: it is in the situation, but it is in the situation without any positive determination linked with the situation itself, it is the most anonymous part of the situation, or, if you want, it is inside the situation the most universal part of the situation. And so the possibility of finding it in another and completely other situation is a real possibility. In fact, when there is an event, or a new truth process, which encounters a generic subset of the past, we have precisely the subset itself returning to life, it is a resurrection, really. Ontologically, the signification is that the generic subset can be the subset of another set then the primitive set. And so we have reason to say that very determined sets, like a concrete situation – or some part of it – with very precise sets, with names, which is in knowledge, which is completely linked to a particular culture, and so on, generally will not be included in another world, in another set, in another culture, but if a subset is generic the situation is not the same, a generic subset can be a subset of many different sets.

The next question is of Michail Tegos.

Question 5: Situation and event are more clear cut in Theory of the Subject, where you use the double articulation of place and force and splace and outplace. Force seems like a more dynamic and active concept compared to appearance in Logics of Worlds, in which you say that the actions and passions of the body cannot cause events. Is force not what interrupts repetition? And is rupture not the exterior interiorized in a decision than again projected to the outside? And, finally, can we force the unnamable?

[Badiou]: *Theory of the Subject*, which is a book of 1982, was written before the idea of the inclusion of the event in the process of a truth, I was in a more structural position. In fact *Theory of the Subject* is a book that is between my first structuralism and something different. I can say that in this book there is some dimension of the real – it is distributed between place, which is on the side of the state, on the side of power, and the excess of the place, which is on the side of resistance, fight, contradiction and so on – and that its dialectic is sufficient to explain the birth of some truths, some new political process, for example. But after that there is a change. Today I no longer think that the real forces of a situation can by themselves completely construct an event. There is a necessity for something that would be the play of chance of a situation, of a moment of exceptional combination and antagonistic contradiction.

I propose to you a new notion of force, because an event is composed of elements of the world, and not a rupture in the exterior. No, the rupture is not in the exterior, the rupture is composed of things, of objects and so on – *it is inside the world*! And it is precisely modifications of the manner of these elements' appearance – changes of the intensities of existence, and so on – which determine the event. This change is not the result of pure rational reflection, there is something which depends on circumstance and on chance. And such changes of intensity are changes in the determination of force, naturally – something which was near inexistence in the world forces a strong existence, *that is the point of the event*. And so we cannot say that forces create the event, but rather, that an event changes the forces. After that, the question of force is determinate, it becomes the real determination, but before that we have the problem of the elements of a new force. And in the field of politics, we perfectly know the dialectical relationship between event and the development of new forces.

Without an event there is a slow development of forces, there is their construction and so on, but with an event we have a brutal change of the entirety of the existence of something and the transformation of some inexistent to something that exists maximally, and after that the distribution between places and forces is not the same.

This is from Anders.

Question 6: Dialectical thinking appears to be both a condition and a limit of philosophical thinking. It is like an infinite spiral caught in its two-dimensionality. Where does the third dimension appear, or how to think of philosophy in 3-D, or

multiple dimensions, if that is at all possible? The moment of the
cut before omega, is it a classical or a quantum moment? Could
truth and event be superimposed?

[Badiou]: This is not an easy question, but I can say something
concerning many points. The question of dimensions is very
interesting – it's a spatial image, but its very interesting –
concerning specifically philosophy, because we can define
philosophy in terms of one-dimensional space, two-dimensional
space, three-dimensional or four-dimensional space, all of these
possibilities are open.

You can say that philosophy is in one-dimension if, finally,
philosophy is a mystical experience, because in mysticism we
have, in fact, only one dimension: the fusion of the limit point –
omega – and any number, a fusion between the finite and
infinite. If philosophy is oriented in the direction of mystic
experience, then we can say that the fundamental result is to be
in one-dimension, in one point. The most classical definition of
philosophy is in fact in two-dimensions: it's something of a
dialectical definition. Philosophy here is positioned as something
between being and existence, between the analytical point of
view and the dialectical point of view, between opinion and
truth, and so on. In this conception philosophy is always in a
space where we have the play of two contradictory terms. But
we can also say that philosophy is, in fact, an operation in the
three-dimensions of time – we have said this before: in the
present a new interpretation of the past for a new possibility in
the future. And, finally, we could also define philosophy with
four-dimensions. I have proposed that there are four conditions
of philosophy, and we could take these conditions as the
dimensions of philosophy. The becoming of philosophy, in this
case, takes place in the space of the four conditions. We have
explained that the necessity of beginning philosophy again is
produced by changes in the conditions of philosophy – new

ideas in science, new artistic creations, new revolutions, and so on. And so philosophy is, in some sense, situated in a space with four-dimensions. And so it is possible to propose different determinations of philosophy in different dimensions.

The image of the spiral is, as we know, a Hegelian image, because Hegel established the comparison, the exclusive comparison, between the dialectical movement and the spiral. And the spiral is in a three-dimensional space, and Hegel explains its rhythm in three terms: affirmation, negation and the negation of negation. But we could also say that there are four moments in Hegel, after all. That is my response to the first part of the question.

The last question – can a truth and event be superimposed? Truth and event are superimposed in mystical experience. And that is, maybe, the minimal definition of mystical experience: in that sort of experience there is no difference between the event of the experience and the truth of the experience. And so, yes: it's a possibility that event and truth are superimposed not only in strictly speaking mystical experience, but more generally, as I have said, in the enthusiasm of political revolt, for example. In a political revolt we often have something like the idea that the event is the truth itself. But this – in my conviction – is false… it's the effect of the sublime – to return to the first question – of the sublime dimension of the event. And, certainly, in the effect, in the greatness of the event, we can imagine that the truth is created by the event itself, *but it's not true, it's not true… the event is only the opening of a new possibility, and not in itself the realization of this possibility.* And so a great revolt, a great event, and so on, is only the beginning of the process – which is a process of fidelity, and which is more and more complex, and which demands another ethical point. The first ethical point is the effect of the sublime, the engagement, the transformation, the immediate subjective transformation, and after that fidelity,

the prescription to continue. And so we cannot reduce the
question of truth to the mystical dimension.

The next question is from Aletheia.

*Question 7: Who is the 'we' that must propose the conditions of
a real future?*

[Badiou]: I think that the proposition of the conditions of a real
future has two dimensions. First, as I have said, an event by
itself is, in some sense, a proposition of a real and new future – it
is the creation of a new possibility. And so it is the creation of
the possibility of engagement in the construction of a new truth.
In that sort of situation there is no 'we', there is the event and
everybody must make a choice – to take this chance or to refuse
this proposition. This is the first aspect of the question. The
second is the orientation of a people in the direction of a future,
from the point of view, from the conviction, in fact, that for
many empirical reasons the world as it is is not a good world.
And so the 'we' is not constituted, but is something that is
always very spontaneous. The 'we' is, ultimately, the 'we' of
everybody who thinks that there is a desire for something else
than the world as it is. After that, it is a question of
circumstances, and not a general question. And it is, finally, a
question of organization, of organization and of organizing all
that has become possible in the direction of a real future.

The sense of the question – in my opinion – is the question of
the *avant-garde*: is there an *avant-garde* that would organize the
vision of the conditions of a real future? And so, the 'we' is the
'we' of an *avant-garde* – we surrealists, we will decide the
future of poetry, we communists will decide the future of
society, we scientists will decide the future of mathematics, and
so on. In all such cases we have the idea of a 'we' which is
organized, which is a certain form of organization.

We have a lot of experience concerning this point: we know the results of such attempts to organize an *avant-garde*, as the point which, in some sense, decides the direction of the future, and the results have not always been good – they have, generally speaking, not been good. And so the question of the 'we', of what is the 'we' that we need is a good question. And we can even ask: can it be in the form of the *avant-garde* of the last century? And, if not, what must be the form of this 'we'? It is a good question, an important question.

In fact, we could even define the last century as the century of the *avant-garde*. Across the 20th century the *avant-garde* was a powerful idea: throughout the last century we have attempts to create an *avant-garde* to determine the future, to provoke an event, to create a rupture, and so on, and *not just in politics, not just in politics*. Certainly we have the idea of the *avant-garde* in politics in the form of the Party, but we also find it in art, and also in science. For example, in France there was a group of mathematicians under the name Bourbaki, whose precise project was to organize the new destiny for mathematics. The idea of the *avant-garde* did not exist only in politics, it was a general idea, a general idea of the relationship of the present and the future, of the passage from the present to the future, in fact. The *avant-garde* was something that organized the future in the present. All of that was very important in the last century, and results, finally, are confusing, in some sense.

I think that our problem today – in our different engagements, in politics, in art, in love, and so on – is precisely this: do we accept the classical form of the *avant-garde* as the operator for changing the future? For me, it is an open question. In some sense I think that we cannot completely refuse this idea absolutely, since there is always a moment that requires collective action, and so a collective organization. And so, some organization, some grouping, some collectivity, finally, is

necessary, *absolutely*, and not only in politics. And yet
organizations under the law of the *avant-garde* have had some
dangerous effects. The dangerous effects, I think, were often the
results of these attempts precisely because the future cannot be
prescribed – the future is not merely development, it is not
merely a continuation of the world as it is – because there cannot
be a full prescription, a full provision of something that is in part
composed by chance, there cannot be complete determinate
organization of something which is a mixture of prediction and
chance. After all if the future will be something new, how can
we, how could we, determine it in advance? There is risk…
there is always risk. And so I accept that the question of Aletheia
– who is the 'we' – is a very important question, a timely
question, but also an obscure question. Finally – and we all
know this – in all fields of creativity we can speak of a crisis of
the 'we', that is, of a crisis of subjectivity, of active subjectivity.
The question, finally, is of the form of organization: what is the
proper form of organization?

You know the 19th century was the century of promise, the
century of the idea of progress, of the birth of a new world, and
the last century was the century of realization, of the will to
effectively realize this promise, it was the century that attempted
to create the new world, and, naturally, also to create a new
humanity. And for this reason it was the century of the *avant-
garde* – *avant-garde* as the form of organization that would
create the future. But the consequences have been terrible –
great destructions – precisely because we had the idea that to
create the new world we must destroy all of the old world. We
can say that the maxim of the last century was: no construction
without destruction… no construction without destruction. The
disposition was that we must accept violence, we must accept
destruction, and must accept war, and so on, because… *to create
the future we have to pay a price*, the price of many millions of

dead men and women… but, if it's a question of a completely
new world, *the price is the price.*

Many, many millions of people thought like this. It was not only
some individuals, some leaders, some thinkers, good or bad,
mad or great. No! It was a popular idea, it was *the common idea.*
And, naturally, there was also the idea that all sacrifices are
possible – and, that they are necessary. It was not only a
readiness to kill the other, but also – and maybe much more –
the readiness to die, the readiness to expose oneself to death. It
was, finally, the extraordinary idea that to create the new world
we can do anything, after all. It was, maybe, the idea of 'by any
means necessary!' But now we are after all of that – since it was
largely a failure, we are after all that. And the temptation today,
and the situation in fact, the dominant situation, is to reject all
that: no violence, no destruction, no crime, no fight, no
possibility… all of that was, finally, a sort of madness, a sort of
exaltation, which created many deaths and destruction, but no
new world. But we must understand that this negation of the past
is, finally, a resignation to accept peacefully the world as it is,
and so it is also a form of renunciation to create a new political
course. If we absolutely reject violence, destruction, fight, if we
reject the 20th century, and also the 19th, we must also say 'no
future, no future is possible!'

And so we are largely between the two – and this is also the
crisis of the 'we' – we are between the terrible experience of
radical destruction to create something new, with a strong *avant-
garde* organized for that, and a resignation to accept the world as
it is, because to really change and destroy this world we must
pay a price which is unacceptable. *This is our subjectivity, this is
the subjectivity of our world.* And so we must propose
something else, we must create something else, and probably
also a new 'we', in order to go beyond this fate, this fate tied to
the crisis of the 'we'. This is our situation: we are between the

old possibility, which is dead, and which we cannot repeat, and an empty wait for a future, a future which, in some sense, is impossible. And so we are between these two possibilities: we cannot repeat, not exactly, but must we continue?

I am not saying that the last century was entirely crime, destruction, and so on, it is much more complex, much more complex. And we have to understand that the will and the conviction of millions and millions of people around the idea of a new world – a conviction which made it possible, in some sense – was something with a terrible greatness, a terrible tragic greatness, but it was not madness, *it was not madness.*

But we are after all of that, and yet we cannot continue the world as it is, anymore than we can repeat. We cannot simply resign to the state of affairs of the world as it is… which is not a good world, not at all…. This is our situation today. And so we must locally transform this situation by our means, we must construct something in the situation, we must construct something, maybe something very small – and we must accept that new experiences are small – but also we must organize something at the scale of the world, of the entire world. I think that today, if we want to do something, this something is international by necessity, that it is its very essence.

Such political experience is in the direction of the future, and the future will be the construction of a new world in the radical sense of a new totality of the world – not 'socialism in one country'. It must begin small, with local experiences, but be global in ideology, it must be international in its nature.

The next question is from Renata.

Question 8: What is the difference between particularity and singularity in their relation to the universal?

[Badiou]: A singularity is in the position of possibly being universal, and reciprocally all that exists which is universal is also singular. So a singularity is a creation in particularity, which is possibly universal. And so the relationship between singularity and universality can be a relationship of identity: you can propose something like universal singularity. Particularity is not necessarily closed on particularity, it is something in which we can create a universal singularity, but particularity *as such* is the term opposed to universality in the beginning of this dialectic. We have, therefore, two terms which are in contradiction – particularity and universality – and singularity is the third term which is composed of particularity – particularity is what composes singularity – but which can be universal, and so there can be a universal singularity by a creation inside of particularity. The relationship between particularity and universality is a directly dialectical relationship – they are two contradictory terms – but this relationship is also the opposite, because there is always the possibility of the unity of the two by the creation of something which is a universal singularity, or a particularoty which is universal. Another name for this sort of thing is truth.

The next question is from Magnolia.

Question 9: Can you please elaborate on your use of normal and abnormal in the relation of law and subject, and in relation to law and subject. The possibility of abnormality, or of producing a rupture in normality, or in the world as it is appears, is performative, that is, produced by the actions of the individual subject. Is the relation between normality and abnormality a rupture? Does, or can, the rupture undue the conformism of the binary? Can we implement these concepts both or simultaneously in relation to the constitution of individual subjectivity and with regards to political existence?

[Badiou]: Normal is strictly in relationship to a law. There is no
possibility of ontologically defining something as normal. And
so it is always just a prescription and not a state of affairs. And
this is very important because if you think that normal is an
ontological predicate then you are engaged in something very
reactionary, certainly. Why? Because we would then have the
right – the ontological right – to oppress, or to suppress all that is
abnormal. And so, we must accept that normal is a category of
the law in general, that it is a prescriptive category, and *not
ontological*. A law can say that something is not normal, that
something is abnormal, but there is no possibility to transform
this prescription into something of objective or ontological
nature. And so the predicates normal and abnormal depend on
the world as it is, on the prescriptions of the world as it is – it is
not the description of something of objective or intemporal
nature.

Generally the law prescribes as normal something that is
adequate to the organization of the world, and so the prescription
is the prescription of the law of the world as it is. And to be
normal is to be inscribed, correctly, in the law of the world –
there is no other definition of normal. And in the evolution of
society, the evolution of the world as it is – which is not purely
static – there is also a dynamic of the world *as it is*. For example,
the development of capitalism is a real development, and it is the
development of the world as it is. And in the becoming of
societies sometimes the law changes: there can be, and there in
fact is, modification of the law within a world, but such
modifications are not changes of the world, they are
modifications of the law, that is, something small, some small
things, can be modified and modified *continually*, this is certain,
and this modification will be the consequence of some
displacement of the separation of normality and abnormality –
something which was abnormal becomes normal, and the
reverse, naturally. But this is not in itself a change *of the world.*

And when something like a truth is constructed, many of the components will, naturally, be abnormal. And why? Simply because a truth is something absolutely new, and this newness cannot be coded by the existing laws, and yet it is, in some sense, from within the world. Very often, then – if not almost always – there will be something abnormal in a new universality. And this site, this abnormal site can sometimes contribute to the change of the world itself, that is, it can contribute to changing the law. And we must understand, then, that an event and the consequences of an event are not by themselves normal or abnormal – those are just judgments, but with no ontological ground.

I propose – from a properly philosophical position – that we only make very small use of the categories of normality and abnormality, and maybe no use at all, except in the biological or medical fields, where we have a strict definition of the difference between normality and pathology – not abnormality but pathology. And this definition in the work of Canguilhem, for example – to name a philosopher of this question, and who wrote a very interesting book the title of which is *The Normal and the Pathological* – is a supposition defined inside the science, and inside science it is the function of the organism which grounds it. Maybe in this place – and with many precautions – we can sometimes use the opposition between normal and abnormal, but generally speaking I don't know how it is possible to use that sort of opposition as, precisely, a normative one. Normality is a norm, but we could have other norms – fidelity to an event, participation in a truth, a will to a new future, engagement, and so on. And nothing here is normal or abnormal. Nobody is normal, finally – that's a better use of normal, nobody is normal. We are all defined by our specific abnormalities. Let that be the last word for today.

Just one word more: It has really been a pleasure to be with you,
it was a pleasure to speak to you, and it was arduous because it
was work, but it was a pleasant work, and if I am tired it is
because I am also an old man, but I am principally very glad for
this moment with you, and so, thank you

Wolfgang Schirmacher, *editor*

Other books available from Atropos Press

5 *Milton Stories (For the Witty, Wise and Worldly Child)*, Sofia Fasos Korahais

Che Guevara and the Economic Debate in Cuba, Luiz Bernardo Pericás

Grey Ecology, Paul Virilio

heart, speech, this, Gina Rae Foster

Follow Us or Die, Vincent W.J., van Gerven Oei

Just Living: Philosophy in Artificial Life. Collected Works Volume 1, Wolfgang Schirmacher

Laughter, Henri Bergson

Pessoa, The Meaphysical Courier, Judith Balso

Philosophical Essays: from Ancient Creed to Technological Man, Hans Jonas

Philosophy of Culture, Schopenhauer and Tradition, Wolfgang Schirmacher

Talking Cheddo: Teaching Hard Kushitic Truths Liberating PanAfrikanism, Menkowra Manga Clem Marshall

Teletheory, Gregory L. Ulmer

The Tupperware Blitzkrieg, Anthony Metivier

Vilém Flusser's Brazilian Vampyroteuthis Infernalis, Vilém Flusser

New Releases from Atropos Press

Beyond Reflection, Anders Kolle

HARDSCAPE/ABC, Andrew Spano

Hermeneutics of New Modernism, Lisa Paul Streitfeld

The Image Is Crisis, Nancy Jones

Languages of Resistance, Maya Nitis

Nanotexts, Tony Prichard

Media, Meaning, & the Legitimation Problem from the Eradication of the Meta Narrative to the Present, Gregory O'Toole

Media Psychology, Matthew Tyler Giobbi

On Techne of Authority: Political Economy in a Digital Age, G. M. Bell

On Leaving: Poetry, Daesthetics, Timelessness, Lori Martindale

On Fidelity; Or, Will You Still Love Me Tomorrow..., Jeremy Fernando

Surfgeist: Narratives of Epic Mythology in New Media, Peggy Ann Bloomer

www.ingramcontent.com/pod-product-compliance
Lightning Source LLC
Chambersburg PA
CBHW070345090426
42733CB00009B/1294

* 9 7 8 1 9 4 0 8 1 3 8 6 8 *